At Issue

Food Insecurity

Other Books in the At Issue Series:

At Issue

I Food Insecurity

Louise I. Gerdes, Book Editor

GREENHAVEN PRESS
A part of Gale, Cengage Learning

GALE
CENGAGE Learning·

Detroit • New York • San Francisco • New Haven, Conn • Waterville, Maine • London

Elizabeth Des Chenes, *Director, Publishing Solutions*

© 2012 Greenhaven Press, a part of Gale, Cengage Learning

Gale and Greenhaven Press are registered trademarks used herein under license.

For more information, contact:
Greenhaven Press
27500 Drake Rd.
Farmington Hills, MI 48331-3535
Or you can visit our Internet site at gale.cengage.com

For product information and technology assistance, contact us at

Gale Customer Support, 1-800-877-4253
For permission to use material from this text or product, submit all requests online at www.cengage.com/permissions

Further permissions questions can be emailed to permissionrequest@cengage.com

Articles in Greenhaven Press anthologies are often edited for length to meet page require-ments. In addition, original titles of these works are changed to clearly present the main thesis and to explicitly indicate the author's opinion. Every effort is made to ensure that Greenhaven Press accurately reflects the original intent of the authors. Every effort has been made to trace the owners of copyrighted material.

Cover image copyright © Images.com/Corbis.

LIBRARY OF CONGRESS CATALOGING-IN-PUBLICATION DATA

Food insecurity / Louise I. Gerdes, book editor.
    p. cm. -- (At issue)
  Includes bibliographical references and index.
  ISBN 978-0-7377-5570-1 (hbk.) -- ISBN 978-0-7377-5571-8 (pbk.)
  1. Food security. 2. Food supply. I. Gerdes, Louise I., 1953-
  HD9000.5.F5952 2012
  363.8--dc23

            2012003817

Printed in the United States of America
1 2 3 4 5 6 7 16 15 14 13 12

Contents

Introduction

Of the approximately 7 billion people who populate the world, nearly 1 billion went hungry in 2010, according to the World Hunger Education Service. Indeed, most experts agree that food insecurity—the lack of consistent and reliable access to food—is a serious global problem. A proverb suggests, "A hungry man is an angry man." In truth, writes Lester R. Brown, founder of the Earth Policy Institute and author of several books on food security and sustainable development, "Food insecurity may soon eclipse terrorism as the overriding concern of national governments."[1] Most experts agree that agricultural practices and policies, the current global economic crisis, and a significant increase in the price of food have been devastating for poor people in developing countries who live on $1.25 a day or less. However, there is significant debate over what led to these conditions and how best to address them. One controversy that is reflective of these debates is the broader question of whether enough food can in fact be sustainably produced to feed the world.

Environmentalists claim that the earth's available resources will soon outstrip the world's growing need for food. They assert that by 2050, the world's population will increase by at least two billion—doubling the demand. Agriculture already consumes the largest percentage of the earth's land surface. Increasing the amount of food produced by expanding the amount of land farmed would risk further destruction of the environment, they argue, and would thus be counterproductive. Indeed, claims Jonathan Foley, director of the Institute on the Environment at the University of Minnesota, "by clearing tropical forests, farming marginal lands, and intensifying industrial farming in sensitive landscapes, humankind has made

---

1. Lester R. Brown. *Outgrowing the Earth: The Food Security Challenge in an Age of Falling Water Tables and Rising Temperatures.* New York: W.W. Norton, 2005.

agriculture the planet's dominant environmental threat."[2] Agriculture is also the greatest source of greenhouse gas emissions—about 35 percent of the carbon dioxide, methane, and nitrous oxide released. "That is more than the emissions from worldwide transportation (including all cars, trucks and planes) or electricity generation,"[3] Foley maintains. To feed the world without further damaging the planet will require a shift in agricultural practices, not an increase in the land farmed, he concludes.

Adding to the problem is the distribution of agricultural production. Only 60 percent of the world's crops are produced to feed people. Of the remainder, 5 percent is produced for biofuels and industrial products and 35 percent is produced for animal feed. "Feeding crops to animals," Foley reasons, "reduces the world's potential food supply."[4] Indeed, some environmentalists blame the problem of food insecurity in part on the protein-rich, meat diets enjoyed by people in the developed world. They fear that as other nations develop, the shift to a more protein rich diet will make it difficult to meet the world's growing demand for food. In fact, experts claim that 30 kilograms of grain are needed to produce one kilogram of edible beef. Chicken and pork are somewhat more efficient. "No matter how you slice it, though, grain-fed meat production systems are a drain on the global food supply," Foley claims. Thus, he and other analysts argue that in order to increase food security, there needs to be a shift away from meat consumption. According to Peter Timmer of the Center for Global Development, "There's still plenty of food for everyone, but only if everyone eats a grain and legume-based diet."[5]

2. Jonathan A. Foley, "Can We Feed the World and Sustain the Planet?" *Scientific American*, October 12, 2011.
3. *Ibid.*
4. *Ibid.*
5. "Asian Rice Crises Puts 10 Million or More at Risk: Q&A with Peter Timmer," Center for Global Development, April 21, 2008. www.cgdev.org.

Other analysts believe that advances in agricultural technology can sustainably produce enough food to feed the world without changing the Western diet. They argue that human ingenuity has improved food production in the past and can do so in the future. These advocates cite twentieth-century improvements during the Green Revolution. Between the late 1940s and the 1970s, Western research led to significant crop-yield increases. Agricultural technology advocates argue that agricultural research and advancement is key. In fact, maintains Marcus Alley, professor of agriculture at Virginia Tech and president of the American Society of Agronomy, improvements are already available. "We have better varieties of seeds [and] methods to control pests,"[6] he claims. For Alley, "the issue is implementation of these technologies."[7] While there is plenty of arable land, agriculture improvement advocates argue, local barriers prevent farmers from farming the land: obstacles such as poverty, unstable governments, and barriers to getting loans block the development of land for farming. "Potentially, can we feed everybody? Of course we can,"[8] claims Ray Cesca, president of the World Agricultural Forum. Indeed, the mission of the forum is to bring together experts and resources to improve world agriculture and reduce global food insecurity.

While agreeing that agricultural improvements will help reduce food insecurity, some commentators claim that implementation policies must help farmers produce locally. In their view, the problem of food insecurity in many developing nations is not simply a lack of agricultural technology but a shift away from local food production and distribution. Over the past twenty years, the world's food system has shifted to a global market. Many countries produce large quantities of a few crops for export and are dependent on imports for their own

6. *Ibid.*
7. *Ibid.*
8. *Ibid.*

food. As a result, these analysts assert, some nations do not produce enough food to feed their own people. Wealthy nations with industrial agricultural practices often subsidize their own farmers who can sell exports below cost, often to the detriment of poorer nations, they maintain. Farmers in developing countries lose their local markets, grow even poorer, and risk greater food insecurity when imports are unavailable or too costly, these analysts reason. "The idea that you should import everything that you can buy cheaper from abroad means that you lose your ability to provide your own staples,"[9] claims Thomas Dobbs, a South Dakota State University economics professor. "Ironically, this is something the United States would never do,"[10] he asserts. Local market farming, what some call food sovereignty, is gaining more support. Indeed, the United Nations and the World Bank, which lends money to promote economic growth in the developing world, have begun to show interest in local agricultural production policies.

Globalization advocates counter that global markets help developing nations create modern economies. "What developing countries need is to develop, not to have their present conditions of life and work preserved like a museum exhibit."[11] Those who support global markets argue that global, not local production reduces food insecurity. According to Brian Wright, professor of agriculture and resource economics at the University of California, Berkeley, "globalization is what stops famines."[12] He and others argue that bad weather or poor agricultural policy decisions can lead to food shortages. "But if you have another place to get food, you have a safety net,"[13] Wright reasons. Responding to claims that the United

---

9. *Ibid.*
10. *Ibid.*
11. Janet Daley, "Forget Fairtrade—Only Free Trade Can Help Poor," *Daily Telegraph* [UK], February 25, 2008.
12. Quoted in Marcia Clemmitt, *supra.*
13. *Ibid.*

States has a competitive advantage over developing nations, Bob Young, chief economist for the American Farm Bureau, argues that American farmers face greater restrictions and tariffs than those in the developing world. While the United States imposes a tariff of about 12 percent, the average tariff faced by US farmers is about 62 percent. Moreover, US farmers face stricter food-safety and environmental regulations and need subsidies to offset these costs.

Clearly, the causes of food insecurity and how best to address the problem remain contentious issues. "I always tell [food] producers that this whole thing is not rocket science—it's far more complicated,"[14] claims US Department of Agriculture supervisory plant physiologist, Jerry L. Hatfield. Indeed, commentators continue to contest whether changes in land use policies, a shift to a grain-based diet, the development of agricultural technology, or a return to local food production will help sustainably feed the world's growing population, thus reflecting the problem's complexity. The authors in the following volume, *At Issue: Food Insecurity*, contest these and other issues as the debate continues. As the world's population grows, so grows the urgent need for answers.

14. *Ibid.*

1

Food Insecurity: An Overview

Fred Powledge

Fred Powledge, a science writer and editor, specializes in biodiversity and other environmental issues, writing articles for publications such as New Yorker, Nation, *and* BioScience.

Food security—equal and consistent access to food by all people—is at risk. Indeed, rising food prices have increased the threat of hunger among the world's poorest people. As the population increases, more people need food. Some predict that climate change will add to the problem, especially in Africa and Southeast Asia where weather has a dramatic impact on key crops. Biotechnology advocates believe genetically engineered (GE) crops will better withstand extreme weather. However, opponents believe biotechnology's impact remains too uncertain and hurts poor farmers who must pay large corporations for GE seeds. The diversion of land to grow crops for biofuels may also increase food insecurity, as did the shift to protein diets in wealthier nations. The poor economic climate has reduced funds for artificial research, so how policymakers will respond remains unclear.

In a world where "security" has lately taken on great significance, it should come as no surprise that "food security" is firmly established in the vocabulary of policy and science. The expression has been defined and used for years, perhaps most succinctly by the United Nations' (UN) Food and Agriculture

Fred Powledge, "Food, Hunger, and Insecurity: Of the World's Current Population of 6.8 billion, 5 Billion Are Living at Levels of Poverty That Deprive Them of Their Basic Needs, and More Than 1 Billion Are Going Hungry," *BioScience*, vol. 60, no. 4, April 2010, pp. 260–265. All rights reserved. Reproduced with permission.

Organization (FAO): "Food security means access by all people at all times to the food needed for a healthy life."

Four Pillars of Food Security

The term is also defined by its opposite, food insecurity, in which some or all of food security's "four pillars," as described by the FAO, are missing: availability, access, utilization, and stability. All four pillars were cracked and sagging in 2007 and 2008 when rising food costs affected millions of people around the world, many of them desperately poor. Deadly food riots ensued in 22 nations and placed hunger at the top of the global agenda.

It hasn't stayed there, however: Jacques Diouf, head of the FAO, told delegates at a 2009 World Food Summit that "unfortunately such interest seems to be waning as other issues are coming to the forefront of the international agenda, although all the heavy clouds that led to the previous crisis are again accumulating in the skies." There have been cloudy days before, but oftentimes they have given way to the sunshine of innovations and discoveries. The Green Revolution of the 1960s, which headed off starvation in Asia and South Asia by introducing specially bred rice and maize, is a celebrated example.

But the Green Revolution created environmental problems of its own, and it was not a lasting solution. Even the late Norman E. Borlaug, who conceived and managed the revolution, called it "a temporary success in man's war against hunger and deprivation." It was, he said when accepting the 1970 Nobel Peace Prize for his work, only "a breathing space" that would prove "ephemeral" within the following three decades unless humankind could think up better solutions, as well as curb "the frightening power of human reproduction." That was four decades ago, when Earth's population was half its present size. And as the problem of hunger grows, so does science's need to understand how to cope with it.

Sounding the Alarm

In October 2009, three respected international organizations released their fourth annual *Global Hunger Index*, a grim set of data (current to 2007). After some progress in reducing the scourge in the 1980s and first half of the 1990s, the report said, hunger was back on the rise. Twenty-nine countries have "levels of hunger that are alarming or extremely alarming." South Asia and sub-Saharan Africa are worst off. And after decades of progress against malnutrition, the number of its victims is rising.

The future doesn't look all that promising. Reports and proclamations of all sorts, some including deadlines by which hunger should be eased or erased, have reached and passed their sell-by dates—yet the world still needs to be fed. The United Kingdom's Royal Institute of International Affairs (also known as Chatham House), the United Kingdom's Royal Society, and the US National Research Council have produced heavy-duty reports viewing the present and future with alarm.

Despite the obvious precariousness of the world's food supply and accessibility, and widespread belief that responsible policymakers relying on scientific research can play huge parts in solving the dilemma, the study of food sometimes is treated as an unpopular relative by the rest of science. Agriculture and its constant companions hunger, malnutrition, and disease have consistently been left out of many scientific discussions. The scientists who study agriculture have their meetings and journals and land-grant colleges, and the other sciences have theirs. The list of papers scheduled for presentation at annual meetings of many scientific associations will have a few items discussing agriculture, but not many. . . .

The Population Problem

There is broad agreement on the big problems to be faced. One issue, though not one many governments wish to talk about, is population—the "frightening power" against which

Borlaug warned. Population growth, even at its current reduced rate of increase, figures into every other issue of food
security, for the simple reason that more mouths need more
food. Much more: The FAO has estimated that if food production is to meet the needs of a world population of 9.1 billion, which is predicted by the year 2050, it must expand by
70 percent worldwide and double in the developing countries.
The usual shorthand holds that 5 billion of the world's current 6.8 billion are living at levels that deprive them of some
of their basic needs, and more than 1 billion are going hungry.

---

*Population growth ... figures into every other issue of
food security, for the simple reason that more mouths
need more food.*

The Impact of Climate Change

There are educated predictions about which regions and crops
will suffer most from temperature rises, erratic precipitation
patterns, and the other anticipated effects of climate change.
There is agreement that southern Africa may lose a big part of
its maize crop unless agriculture somehow adapts. A similar
crisis may face the rice-growing areas of Southeast Asia.

Despite their decades of experience with crop yield and
climate, agricultural researchers have had a hard time making
their case at global climate change summits. When the world's
climate experts and some political leaders gathered last December in Copenhagen for the UN Climate Change Conference, prominent agricultural scientists tried to get their concerns before the climate scientists. But scant attention was
paid to issues of food security and the need for adaptation.

In the language of crop scientists, adaptation means finding the genes within the genetic variability of domesticated
food plants and animals, as well as their wild relatives, that

can withstand the assumed rigors of climate change, and then breeding those genes into the plants that farmers and consumers want. In the past, this breeding for adaptation, such as the ability to withstand drought, saline soils, cold or heat, or heavy precipitation, has been a slow process. Biotechnology promises to speed things up, but it is a highly controversial method, not least because it raises issues of intellectual property rights and the property rights of indigenous farmers, who may have selected landraces [local varieties of animal or plant species] and wild relatives for centuries.

At the International Crops Research Institute for the Semi-Arid Tropics (ICRISAT) in Patancheru, India, scientists work on crops such as millet, sorghum, pigeon pea, chickpea, and groundnuts—foods eaten by the poorest people on Earth and cultivated by them on the driest and poorest soils. The ICRISAT crops have been selected by farmers and nature over centuries to withstand drought and high temperatures. William Dar, ICRISAT's director general, says the present research strategy is to improve the crops' heat tolerance even further, using germplasm stored in the center's gene bank. Pearl millet and sorghum have high levels of salinity tolerance, another sought-after trait, in some cases at temperatures of more than 42 degrees Celsius.

Much of this research depends on painstaking recordkeeping that describes in detail the conditions under which their accessions were collected—latitude and longitude, temperature, elevation, and the day length that is necessary for growth and seed setting. A well-run gene bank—ICRISAT and other members of the international agricultural research community qualify—is likely to be on the front lines of adaptation to climate change and the need to increase yield.

Plant "breeding," on the other hand, means using the methods of finding and crossing varieties with desired characteristics—a time-consuming process. Geoffrey Hawtin has practiced agricultural research and policymaking at a number of the international centers, most notably the International Plant Genetic Resources Institute (now named Bioversity International) in Rome, where he was director general. "My concern about plant breeding," he says, "is that it takes on average 10 years, and up to 15 years, from the time you make a cross to the time you release the new variety and distribute it to farmers. That means that we actually need to be breeding today for the expected climate in 2020." That's a difficult task indeed, especially with the cutbacks that donors have made in their funding for international research.

Today, Hawtin says, genetic conservators are doing less collecting of the old varieties of food plants in favor of looking for a food plant's wild relatives. "Very often it is those crops' wild relatives that are going to have more interesting and radically different genes than you might find within the cultivated species"—genetic characteristics that may come in handy in a warmer, drier future, or that might produce greater yields to feed a swollen population. "And so there's an increasing interest in looking not just at the margins of where the crops grow but at the margins of where some of the wild species grow, to look for some extreme adaptations that could be hopefully readily transferred to the cultivated species." By "readily," Hawtin means free of any need for genetic engineering. "You might just be able to make regular crosses of some sort to get the genes transferred in a more or less conventional way."

The Biotechnology Controversy

Climate change and population growth may be the most dramatic challenges to agriculture these days, but there are others. One is a widespread, boundless faith in the miracles that can be wrought by technology. Today, that means biotechnology—the kind that produces genetically modified (GM) organisms. Biotech is controversial, one reason being that the ownership of much GM plant material is concentrated in multinational companies and costs farmers money every time they plant it.

While the discussion of GM crops may best be described as a shouting match in much of the more-developed world, in Africa it is a component of a polite discussion of food and the future. Part of that discussion is being carried out by Calestous Juma, a celebrated student of development and agriculture in the African world and elsewhere, and now director of the Science, Technology, and Globalization Project at Harvard's Kennedy School of Government. Juma collaborated with Ismail Serageldin on a report titled *Freedom to Innovate: Biotechnology in Africa's Development* (2007). The report discusses what African states need in order to build their capacity to use biotechnology "to improve agricultural productivity, public health, industrial development, economic competitiveness, and environmental sustainability."

There are way too many unanswered questions on the ecological and health safety of [genetically modified organisms] that still need to be answered.

Juma compares potential advances in biotechnology with those occurring in Africa in communications. "Africa is already benefiting from advances in telecommunications," he says. "Not long ago, mobile phones were considered to be toys for elites in industrialized countries. They have now become indispensable in all aspects of social and economic life. There is mounting evidence that biotechnology will do for agriculture in these countries what mobile phones have done for communication."

Will biotech in Africa run into some of the same opposition it has faced in Europe and other parts of the North? "Only time will tell," Juma replies. "European reactions were guided by domestic political considerations. Africa has its own political challenges, too, and they will play out. But the outcomes will depend on whether the products confer real benefits."

Skepticism About GM Food

Hans Herren, who formerly ran the Nairobi-based International Centre of Insect Physiology and Ecology, and who now heads the Millennium Institute, is one of the authors of a landmark study of global agriculture. The *International Assessment of Agricultural Knowledge, Science, and Technology for Development* (IAASTD) is an examination of the past and current state of global agriculture and a look at its future, with suggestions for improvement. Herren is deeply skeptical of the promise of genetically modified organisms (GMOs).

"As we wrote in the IAASTD report," Herren says, "we need a new paradigm. . . . GMOs are part of the business as usual, [along with] synthetic fertilizers and large-scale, monoculture-based agriculture. All these have no future in a world that is constrained in terms of energy and nonrenewable resources. . . . There is little need for genetic manipulation when farmers have the means to manage their farms according to agro-ecological principles. It has been shown many times over that organic agriculture, which regenerates the soil, can feed the world today and tomorrow; actually, it's the only way to do so in the medium and long term.

"There are way too many unanswered questions on the ecological and health safety of GMOs that still need to be answered before any sensible decision to grow and eat them could be made."

And then there's the matter of who owns the germplasm in the first place. "Genetic engineering of plants and animals, furthermore, brings with it the intellectual property issue," says Herren. "That is important when we talk about food as a human right. . . . How can the basic need of humanity, which has been developed with great labor and testing by farmers and nature over the eons, now become the property of a few?"

The IAASTD report was the result of a three-year collaboration drawing on the expertise of sonic 400 individuals, including representatives from 110 governments, numerous nongovernmental organizations, consumer groups, scientists, and others, organized by World Bank, the FAO, and other UN agencies. Basically, the report calls for a new look at the world's agricultural development and sustainability goals to place them in a context of uncertainties about sustainability, environmental conditions, energy, disease, cost of food, and social inequities of all sorts. These are areas global agriculture has generally avoided.

The final report was endorsed by 58 governments; leaders of Australia, Canada, and the United States were not among them. Herren says even his alma mater, the Consultative Group on International Agricultural Research (CGIAR), condemned the report as unscientific.

A Lack of Research Money

As governments have begun to feel the financial pinches of recent years, their investment in agricultural research has declined. The United States is close to the bottom of world powers in providing a percentage of its gross national product as official development assistance to needy countries.

Partly because of the donor drought, CGIAR, the world's premier international agricultural research organization, has plunged itself into a lengthy reform effort that clearly is aimed at extracting more money from donors, many of which are the development agencies of national governments. Once complete, this "change management initiative," as it is called, would allow the 15 CGIAR centers to continue their work of improving the developing world's access to its basic foods—rice, wheat, maize, potato, sweet potato, yam, cassava, beans, coconut, banana, and plantain—as well as fish and aquaculture products, water, livestock, oil crops, fruits and vegetables, and forestry products.

So far, the reform is still a work in progress, but some positive early indicators have emerged. The Gates Foundation will contribute some of its funds and, according to some reports, be rewarded with a decision-making role in CGIAR. The 15 research centers will join a consortium that will run "mega-programs." Currently, each center has its own programs and must prevail upon donors for funds to run them. The new setup will draw on a common research fund.

The Effects of Malnutrition

One of the more touching faces of food insecurity is malnutrition, especially that affecting children. Television viewers in the wealthier North have helped to keep this issue alive with their financial donations, but the recession may cause pictures of emaciated and dying babies to lose some impact.

The FAO says that one out of every five people in the developing world is "chronically undernourished," a category that extends not just to babies but also to the elderly, pregnant women (who produce offspring with low weight and low weight gain), and children and adolescents (who may be stunted and suffer from reduced mental capacity). Many of the problems of malnourishment could easily and cheaply be avoided if their victims received adequate quantities of micronutrients, such as iodized salt and vitamin A.

A Need for Useful Land

Earth is running low on available, agriculturally useful land, and there's competition for what is left, from urbanization, forest conservation, the need for carbon sequestration, and other competitors. Jonathan Foley, who directs the Institute on the Environment at the University of Minnesota, has written of his fear that with all the current attention on climate change, "we are neglecting another, equally inconvenient truth: *that we now face a global crisis in land use and agriculture that could undermine the health, security, and sustainability of our civilization*" (emphasis in original). The future of civilization, Foley says, "requires that we simultaneously address the grand challenges of climate change *and* land use, ultimately finding new ways to meet the needs of our economy, our security, and the environment. Anything less will be a complete catastrophe."

Growing crops for fuel squanders land, water, and energy reseources vital for the production of food for human consumption.

The Shift to Biofuels

A potentially huge competitor for agricultural land is biofuel production. Promoted as a way to reduce the industrialized world's dependence on fossil fuels to run its industries and automobiles, this relatively new technology depends in part on growing biofuel crops—inedible by humans, for the most part—on land that once produced food (or on land converted from forest). The biofuel picture is developing rapidly; new sources of fuel, such as recycled grease and algae grown in abandoned mines, are being touted as sources that wouldn't disturb agriculture.

David Pimentel is doubtful, however. The Cornell University agricultural scientist does not trust the enthusiastic reports of biofuel's advantages, and he thinks the move toward such fuels is already taking useful farmland out of production in the United States. (He feels much the same way about GM foods.) Pimentel and others published a critique of biofuels in 2009, when most discussions of biofuel concerned maize, in which they argued that "growing crops for fuel squanders land, water, and energy resources vital for the production of food for human consumption. Using corn for ethanol increases the price of US beef, chicken, pork, eggs, breads, cereals, and milk more than 20 percent to 30 percent." And devoting land to growing biofuels "exacerbates the problem of malnourishment worldwide" by turning much-needed food grain into biofuel.

The willingness of scientists and policymakers to explore the crisis's connections as never before . . . is unprecedented.

Moving to Protein and Seafood

As nations and people move from the ranks of desperately poor toward affluence, their tastes change. As they shift from rice and beans to the beef, pork, and chicken consumed by the wealthier world, the agricultural balance sheet changes. Commercial, or "factory," meat production requires large quantities of land, grain, and water; one projection (from Pimentel) is that beef cattle production requires an energy input to protein output of 54 to 1.

Increased consumption of fish is a part of the protein shift, too, especially in China. Also, the promotion of fish as part of a healthy diet, says the FAO, is "changing food preferences in many industrial countries." Per capita fish consumption has increased, notes the *Millennium Ecosystem Assessment* (MEA), at the same time that fish stocks have declined in all oceans to the point that they are "near or exceeding their maximum sustainable level of exploitation."

Examinations of the global agricultural situation often overlook aquatic products, but these foods are significant. According to the FAO, some 520 million people depend on fisheries and aquaculture as a source of protein and income. For the poorest 400 million of them, half or more of their protein and minerals come from fish. Climate change and the food system's other stresses affect these people, and their diets, as they do others—with the added worries that their sources of food are endangered by overfishing and habitat loss.

Any Signs of Hope?

Food insecurity is not likely to go away or be forgotten after the next election or global financial upswing. Mark W. Rosegrant and Sarah A. Cline, in a December 2003 *Science* piece, wrote that food insecurity "will remain a worldwide concern for the next 50 years and beyond," driven by declining crop yields, increasing water scarcity, climate change, HIV/AIDS, and more.

The flurry of attention that currently is being paid to the notion of a global food crisis is one hopeful sign, say those who worry about it, for it aims a spotlight at a crisis that often is ignored. The willingness of scientists and policymakers to explore the crisis's connections as never before—links to environment, climate, ecology, finance—is unprecedented. The MEA is a significant example, as is the IAASTD report.

Prominent in the 2009 IAASTD report is reliance on the term "multi-functionality." The multisyllabic term is used by the authors "to express the inescapable interconnectedness of agriculture's different roles and functions." Agriculture, says the report, "is a multi-output activity producing not only commodities . . . but also noncommodity outputs such as environmental services, landscape amenities, and cultural heritages" that must be included in any effort to feed the world in global terms, not national or regional. That's a tall order for a first world of well-fed people who are accustomed to thinking of food as almost free and ever-abundant—or to not having to think of food at all.

But will the policymakers pay attention, or will it take more rioting in the streets?

2

Food Insecurity Among American Children Has Serious Consequences

John Cook and Karen Jeng

John Cook, professor of pediatrics at Boston University School of Medicine, is a nationally recognized expert on child hunger. Karen Jeng is a research fellow at Boston University School of Public Health and Children's HealthWatch, a pediatric research center that monitors the impact of economic conditions and public policy decisions on the health and well-being of children.

Food insecurity among America's children results in dramatic health and economic costs. Hungry children are sick more often and more likely to visit the hospital—these costs result in higher health insurance rates and taxes. Health problems also carry into adulthood, which leads to additional health care costs, absenteeism, and poor performance at work. Hungry children experience lower academic achievement and have social and behavioral problems that carry over into the workforce. As a result, America's workforce is less competitive and less productive. Since the nation's growth depends on the health of America's children, eliminating child hunger should be a priority. Like a vaccine, good nutrition can prevent health problems and increase American productivity with the cooperation of public and private food assistance programs.

Mﾠore than 12 million children under the age of eighteen in the United States are food insecure—unable to consistently access adequate amounts of nutritious food necessary for a healthy life. More than three million children under the age of five are food insecure.

What does this mean for the United States? The costs of child food insecurity are great. Food insecurity not only affects a child and his or her family, but is a problem that impacts society economically through a variety of channels. By affecting a child's health, education, and workforce and job readiness, the impacts of child hunger are more far reaching than one might anticipate.

Child Hunger Is a Health Problem

Hungry children are sick more often, and more likely to have to be hospitalized (the costs of which are passed along to the business community as insurance and tax burdens)[.]

Hungry children suffer growth impairment that precludes their reaching their full physical potential[.]

Hungry children incur developmental impairments that limit their physical, intellectual and emotional development.

Child Hunger Is an Educational Problem

Hungry children ages 0–3 years cannot learn as much, as fast, or as well, because chronic undernutrition and toxic stress harm their cognitive development during this critical period of rapid brain growth. This actually changes the fundamental neurological architecture of the brain and central nervous system[.]

Hungry children do more poorly in school and have lower academic achievement because they are not well prepared for school and cannot concentrate[.]

Hungry children have more social and behavioral problems because they feel bad, have less energy for complex social interactions, and cannot adapt as effectively to environmental stresses.

Child Hunger Is a Workforce and Job Readiness Problem

Workers who experienced hunger as children are not as well prepared physically, mentally, emotionally or socially to perform effectively in the contemporary workforce[.]

Workers who experienced hunger as children create a workforce pool that is less competitive, with lower levels of educational and technical skills, and seriously constrained human capital.

[T]he results of chronic undernutrition contribute to high health care costs throughout life.

The Costs of Child Food Insecurity

Child hunger leads to greater health care costs for families and employers.

Short-term: hungry children have greater odds of being hospitalized, and the average pediatric hospitalization costs approximately $12,000.

Long-term: the results of chronic undernutrition contribute to high health care costs throughout life.

Child hunger leads to greater absenteeism, presenteeism (present but not fully productive) and turnover in the work environment, all of which are costly for employers. Child sick days are linked to parent employee absences, for instance.

Prevention Programs

Child hunger is totally preventable and unnecessary in the United States.

The federally-funded nutrition assistance infrastructure works: nutrition assistance programs provide the first-line defense against child hunger, if adequately funded.

Good nutrition is just like a good antibiotic or vaccine in preventing illness. The Supplemental Nutrition Assistance Program (formerly The Food Stamp Program), WIC [Special Supplemental Nutrition Program for Women, Infants and Children], the National School Lunch and Breakfast Programs, Child and Adult Care Food Program, TEFAP [The Emergency Food Assistance Program] and other public nutrition assistance programs are good medicine, but the dose is often not strong enough and the prescription is not for a long enough time period. Many families cannot overcome the barriers to access to these services which are crucial for health.

Private food assistance programs guarantee that no child falls through the cracks by buttressing, complementing and supporting the public nutrition infrastructure—the food bank network makes up the difference in dose required and duration for which it is needed to cure the serious health problem of child hunger.

Working together, in mutually supportive partnership, the national public and private food assistance systems can prevent and eradicate the unnecessary health problem of childhood hunger, if we the people choose to do so.

Investing in Our Nation's Children

The nation's economic growth depends on the well-being of our children.

By investing in the health of our nation's children, we ensure that our economy will continue to grow. The future of our economy is dependent on producing healthy, strong, and well-educated children. America's Business Leaders can play a central role in the nation's economic growth by investing in America's children.

Child hunger can be prevented through advocacy.

It is critical that federal child nutrition programs are strengthened by working to eliminate barriers in accessing these programs, streamlining the administration of these programs, and ensuring that these programs are adequately funded. As Congress prepares for the reauthorization of child nutrition programs, Feeding America and its network of over 200 food banks are advocating for children by working to strengthen the quality and efficiency of all child nutrition programs; reaching more low income children at times when school lunch is not available, such as summertime and weekends; and offering new and innovative approaches to reach children in underserved areas, such as in rural communities.

3

Food Insecurity Is a Cause and Consequence of Armed Conflicts

Saswati Bora, Iride Ceccacci, Christopher Delgado, and Robert Townsend

Saswati Bora and Iride Ceccacci are operations analysts, Christopher Delgado is a strategy and policy adviser, and Robert Townsend is a senior economist in the Agriculture and Rural Development Department of The World Bank, an international financial institute that provides loans to developing countries to reduce poverty and promote trade and investment.

Conflict is both a cause and consequence of food insecurity, which makes helping the poor in developing nations a significant challenge. Research reveals that the potential for conflict grows in nations where greed motivates some groups to control high-value food resources in a way that others perceive to be unfair. This is particularly true in nations that depend on the export of these resources and where the distribution of income is unequal. The fact that conflict itself contributes to food insecurity complicates the problem. Conflict destroys resources needed to produce food, displaces people from their source of food, and diverts agricultural resources to the military. In addition to providing food aid and agricultural investments, strengthening governments and reducing unequal food distribution will help end the conflict and food insecurity cycle.

30

Food security exists when all people, at all times, have physical and economic access to sufficient, safe and nutritious food that meets dietary needs and food preferences for an active and healthy life (FAO) [Food and Agricultural Organization of the United Nations] . . . . It includes the following dimensions:

- availability: the availability of sufficient quantities of appropriate quality;

- access: access by individuals to adequate resources for acquiring appropriate foods for a nutritious diet on a regular basis;

- utilization: utilization of food through adequate diet, clean water, sanitation and health care to reach a nutritional well-being where all physiological needs are met;

- stability: a population, household or individual must have access to food at all times and should not risk losing access as a consequence of sudden shocks or cyclical events.

A Vicious Circle

Problems with any of these dimensions can lead to food insecurity, while the latter has often been associated with outbreaks of social unrest or more severe forms of conflict. On the other hand, situations of conflict have in many instances been a primary cause of interference with one or more of the dimensions of food insecurity. A vicious circle of conflict and food insecurity makes alleviation of poverty in rural areas of the most vulnerable countries especially intractable. The root cause of conflict is often to be found in competition over the factors of food production, primarily land and water, exacerbated by other troubling trends. Having more people to feed, with less land and water, more variable climate, and greater food price volatility increases stress on livelihoods and food systems. Yet countries under the greatest stress in this sense are often the least able to respond.

Unpacking the links between food insecurity and conflict helps identify entry points for dealing with both; it is critical to breaking the vicious circle, especially in rural areas that tend to be poorer and more dependent on agriculture for both food and livelihoods. Food aid is the typical instrument needed to limit the immediate food insecurity impacts of conflict. Besides the clear humanitarian outcome in its own right, it can help provide a better context for resolving other issues of social discontent. Done right, food aid can also assist in better transition to longer-term agricultural productivity growth that will be essential to finding more stable solutions to root causes of conflict in many rural areas. However, even food aid can exacerbate conflict under some situations, and used poorly on a recurring basis, it can also exacerbate some of the root causes of social discontent. In agriculture-based conflict countries, the focus needs to be agricultural productivity growth and food security.

A vicious circle of conflict and food insecurity makes alleviation of poverty in rural areas of the most vulnerable countries especially intractable.

The Motives of War

Studies on the motives of war have found conflict to be closely associated with underlying factors affecting food insecurity.

Political studies of the economic motivations of war have argued that conflict was precipitated in some cases by "*greed*" (the desire to control resources) and in others by "*grievance*" (the perception of unfairness by those receiving the short end of contested resources).

Although most of the studies on greed and grievance have concentrated on non-renewable, non-agricultural resources, high value agricultural resources may also be responsible when competing groups fight over access to land and water sources to produce high value commodities like coffee or cotton. For example, the collapse of coffee prices led to a sudden drop in income for small farmers in Rwanda and contributed to the complex forces of causation that contributed to the 1994 genocide.

Countries dependent on primary commodity exports are especially vulnerable to conflicts. [P.] Collier states that a country that is heavily dependent upon primary commodity exports, with a quarter of its national income coming from them, has a risk of conflict four times greater than one without primary commodity exports.

Poverty, hunger and food insecurity, together with a very unequal distribution of income, land and other material goods, provide a fertile ground for . . . individuals and groups with a desire to cause conflict.

Using rainfall shock as an instrumental variable for economic growth in a sample of African countries, [E.] Miguel[1] (2004) found that rainfall shocks have a dramatic impact on the [S. Satyanath, and E. Sergenti] likelihood of civil war: a five percentage-point negative rainfall shock increases the likelihood of a civil war the following year by nearly one-half. The study found that the impact of economic shocks is approximately the same across countries with a range of different economic, social and political institutional characteristics, suggesting that economic shocks are a critical determinant of civil conflict in Africa. However, [M.] Bruckner and [A.] Ciccone found that the effect of low growth on the likelihood of civil war is significantly weaker in countries with democratic institutions. They note that low growth increases the likeli-

---

1. Rainfall shock is a significant deviation from average annual rainfall in areas where rainfall plays an important role in the harvest and therefore household income.

hood of civil war in autocracies, and conclude that there is interaction between economic and institutional causes of civil war.

The extent to which underlying forces can be politically destabilizing depends on the preexisting political and socioeconomic context. Poverty, hunger and food insecurity, together with a very unequal distribution of income, land and other material goods, provide a fertile ground for grievances that can be exploited by individuals and groups with a desire to cause conflict.

[C.] Vallings and [M.] Moreno-Torres argue that the central driver of fragility is weak state institutions. Poverty is linked to fragility but not all poor areas are necessarily fragile. Fragility can occur when poverty or economic decline are combined with weak state institutions that cannot manage the very real grievances caused by, say, inequitable distribution of resources or unequal access to formal institutions. This means that in fragile states political situations are not strong enough to manage the natural conflicts that occur in society. FAO states that structural factors—such as failed institutions and conflicts over land and resources—are at the root cause of most protracted crises. . . .

Food Insecurity as a Consequence of Conflict

Food shortages or other dimensions of severe food insecurity are an obvious consequence of conflict in many cases. Conflict typically reduces availability, access, and utilization of food. It also leads to poverty, high infant mortality, inequality, and declining per capita incomes. The growth inhibiting impacts of conflict can be observed in the rapid resumption of agricultural growth following peace, as experienced in Mozambique.

Conflict destroys land, water, biological, and social resources for food production. Thirty million people in more than 60 countries were displaced or had their livelihoods destroyed by conflict every year in the 1990s. FAO has estimated losses of almost $52 billion in agricultural output through conflict in Sub-Saharan Africa between 1970 to 1997, a figure equivalent to 75 percent of all official development assistance received by the conflict-affected countries. Estimated losses for all developing countries averaged $4.3 billion per year—enough to have raised the food intake of 330 million undernourished people to minimum required levels.

One of the most direct effects of conflict on food security is the displacement of people. In 2001, there were more than 12 million refugees, 25 million internally displaced people (IDPs) and an unknown number of people trapped in combat zones. Most of these need temporary food assistance until they can return to their homes or find new livelihoods. Contributing to meeting the food needs of refugees places an additional burden on recipient communities where food security is already marginal leading to sometimes acute food shortages. Refugees fleeing fighting in northern Chad upset markets in western Darfur during the drought years 1983–85, transforming that food shortage into a famine.

Food shortages or other dimensions of severe food insecurity are an obvious consequence of conflict. . . .

The Conflict Trap

The use of hunger as a weapon ("food war"), which includes selective distribution of food to favor populations in pro-government areas, is implicated in the famines of the 1980s and 1990s in Africa, and in chronic underproduction and food insecurity in post-conflict economies in Africa, Asia and Latin America. The Sudan civil war (1983–84) arose as Southern groups rebelled to assert economic and political rights being denied by the Northern-dominated government. Hunger was used as a deliberate weapon of war leading to almost 7 percent in one camp dying each week. The ensuing famine had its origin in the civil war—raiding of cattle, combined with scorched earth tactics, disrupted economic life and deprived people of assets that normally protected against famine.

Military expenditures lower investments in health, education, agriculture and environmental protection. In the late 1990s and early 2000s, low and middle-income countries devoted nearly 13 percent of government budgets to defense.

Economic sanctions are another potential source of conflict related hunger. For example, after the Gulf War, Iraq faced economic sanctions after years of reliance on external food supplies exchanged for oil revenues. Although essential food was allowed, the poor had less access to food and medicines under sanctions for reasons of both diminished total availability and the distributional policies of the government of the day, and this contributed to significant child mortality.

The impact of conflict on poverty and hunger, in turn, makes conflict more likely. Regression estimates suggest that halving the income of a country is associated with a doubling of the risk of civil war. Conflict is also likely to reoccur generating a "conflict trap" in which countries embark on a downward spiral of increasing impoverishment, hunger and violence. . . .

Recommendations

The key to improving access to food as quickly as possible, while addressing long-term structural problems, is to strengthen local institutions, many times building on informal mechanisms already in place. The current aid architecture also has to be stable and linked to both short and long term agricultural investments that reduce food insecurity and distribute income to the poorest widely. At the same time, current policies at the national, regional and international level can be improved to reduce developing countries' susceptibility to shocks.

4

Diverting Corn and Grain to Biofuels Increases Food Insecurity

Lester R. Brown

Lester R. Brown is president of the Earth Policy Institute, an organization whose mission is to develop a global plan to move the world toward an environmentally and economically sustainable path. Brown is also the author of Plan B 2.0: Rescuing a Planet Under Stress and a Civilization in Trouble.

The United States corn harvest is closely tied to the global food economy. Diverting a significant portion of this crop to produce fuel rather than food will increase food prices in an already volatile food economy. Merging the fuel and food economies risks tying the price of food to fuel—if the price of oil rises, so will the price of food. The billions of people struggling to pay for food will be competing with the millions who want fuel for their cars. This competition could lead to food riots that further disrupt the global economy. Efforts to reduce America's dependence on foreign oil should not lead to greater problems. Rather than subsidize grain-based fuel, policymakers should encourage a shift to more fuel-efficient cars.

The escalating share of the U.S. grain harvest going to ethanol distilleries is driving up food prices worldwide. Investment in fuel ethanol distilleries has soared since gasoline prices jumped at the end of 2005. Once completed, distilleries now under construction could double U.S. ethanol output, turning nearly 30 percent of next year's U.S. grain harvest into fuel for automobiles. This unprecedented diversion of the world's leading grain crop to the production of fuel will affect food prices everywhere, risking political instability.

The U.S. corn crop, accounting for 40 percent of the global harvest and supplying nearly 70 percent of the world's corn imports, looms large in the world food economy. Annual U.S. corn exports of some 55 million tons account for nearly one fourth of world grain exports. The corn harvest of Iowa alone exceeds the entire grain harvest of Canada. Substantially reducing this export flow would send shock waves throughout the world economy.

The Rising Price of Staples

In six or the last seven years, total world grain production has fallen short of use. As a result, world carryover stocks of grain have been drawn down to 57 days of consumption, the lowest level in 34 years. The last time they were this low wheat and rice prices doubled.

Already corn prices have doubled over the last year, wheat futures are trading at their highest level in 10 years, and rice prices are rising. Soybean prices are up by half. If the United States were to suffer intense heat and severe drought this summer in the Corn Belt, rising grain prices could quickly take the world into uncharted territory.

The countries initially hit by rising food prices are those where corn is the staple food. In Mexico, one of more than 20 countries with a corn-based diet, the price of tortillas is up by 60 percent. Angry Mexicans in crowds of up to 75,000 have taken to the streets in protest, forcing the government to institute price controls on tortillas.

Food prices are also rising in China, India, and the United States, countries that contain 40 percent of the world's people. While relatively little corn is eaten directly in these countries, vast quantities are consumed indirectly. The milk, eggs, cheese, chicken, ham, ground beef, ice cream, and yogurt in the typical refrigerator are all produced with corn. In effect, the refrigerator is filled with corn. And the price of every one of these items in the refrigerator is affected by the price of corn.

Rising grain and soybean prices are driving up meat and egg prices in China. January [2007] pork prices were up 20 percent above a year earlier, eggs were up 16 percent, while beef, which is less dependent on grain, was up 6 percent. For China, which suffered the most massive famine in human history in 1959–61, these food price rises could be approaching a politically dangerous level.

In India, the overall food price index in January 2007 was 10 percent higher than a year earlier. The price of wheat, the staple food in northern India, has jumped 11 percent, moving above the world market price.

Merging Food and Fuel Economies

In the United States, the U.S. Department of Agriculture projects that the wholesale price of chicken in 2007 will be 10 percent higher on average than in 2006, the price of a dozen eggs will be up a whopping 21 percent, and milk will be 14 percent higher. And this is only the beginning.

In the past, food price rises have usually been weather related and always temporary. This situation is different. As more and more fuel ethanol distilleries are built, world grain prices are starting to move up toward their oil-equivalent value in what appears to be the beginning of a long-term rise.

The food and energy economies, historically separate, are now merging. In this new economy, if the fuel value of grain exceeds its food value, the market will move it into the energy economy. As the price of oil climbs so will the price of food. If oil jumps from $60 to $80 a barrel, you can bet that your supermarket bills will also go up. If oil climbs to $100, how much will you pay for a dozen eggs?

From an agricultural vantage point, the automotive demand for fuel is insatiable. The grain it takes to fill a 25-gallon tank with ethanol just once will feed one person for a whole year. Converting the entire U.S. grain harvest to ethanol would satisfy only 16 percent of U.S. auto fuel needs.

Since the United States is the leading exporter of grain, shipping more than Canada, Australia, and Argentina combined, what happens to the U.S. grain crop affects the entire world. With the massive diversion of grain to produce fuel for cars, exports will drop. What was for decades the world's breadbasket is fast becoming the U.S. fuel tank.

The grain it takes to fill a 25-gallon tank with ethanol just once will feed one person for a whole year.

The number of hungry people in the world has been declining for several decades, but in the late 1990s the trend reversed and the number began to rise. The United Nations currently lists 34 countries as needing emergency food assistance. Many of these are considered failing states, including Chad, Iraq, Liberia, Haiti, and Zimbabwe. Since food aid programs typically have fixed budgets, if the price of grain doubles, food aid will be reduced by half.

Urban food protests in response to rising food prices in low and middle income countries, such as Mexico, could lead to political instability that would add to the growing list of failing states. At some point, spreading political instability could disrupt global economic progress.

The Ethanol Euphoria

Against this backdrop, Washington is consumed with "ethanol euphoria." President Bush in his [2007] State of the Union address set a production goal for 2017 of 35 billion gallons of alternative fuels, including grain-based and cellulosic ethanol, and fuel from coal. Given the current difficulties in producing cellulosic ethanol at a competitive cost and given the mounting public opposition to coal fuels, which are far more carbon-intensive than gasoline, most of the fuel to meet this goal might well have to come from grain. This could take most of the U.S. grain harvest, leaving little grain to meet U.S. needs, much less those of the hundred or so countries that import grain.

The stage is now set for direct competition for grain between the 800 million people who own automobiles, and the world's 2 billion poorest people. The risk is that millions of those on the lower rungs of the global economic ladder will start falling off as rising food prices drop their consumption below the survival level.

Soaring food prices could lead to urban food riots in scores of lower-income countries that rely on grain imports, such as Indonesia, Egypt, Algeria, Nigeria, and Mexico. The resulting political instability could in turn disrupt the global economy, directly affecting all countries.

We need to make sure that in trying to solve one problem—our dependence on imported oil—we do not create a far more serious one: chaos in the world food economy.

The Alternatives

There are alternatives to this grim scenario. A rise in auto fuel efficiency standards of 20 percent, phased in over the next decade would save as much oil as converting the entire U.S. grain harvest into ethanol.

One option that is gaining momentum is a shift to plug-in hybrids. Adding a second storage battery to a gas-electric hybrid car along with a plug-in capacity so that the batteries can be recharged at night allows most short-distance driving—daily commuting and grocery shopping, for example—to be done with electricity. If this shift were accompanied by investment in hundreds of wind farms that could feed cheap electricity into the grid, then cars could run largely on electricity for the equivalent cost of less than $1 per gallon gasoline.

Ethanol euphoria is not an acceptable substitute for a carefully thought through policy. Do we really want to subsidize a rise in food prices? For Washington, it is time to decide whether to continue with the current policy of subsidizing more and more grain-based fuel distilleries or to encourage a shift to more fuel-efficient cars and a new automotive fuel economy centered on plug-in hybrid cars and wind energy. The choice is between a future of rising world food prices, spreading hunger, and growing political instability, or one of stable food prices, sharply reduced dependence on oil, and much lower carbon emissions.

As the leading grain producer, grain exporter, and ethanol producer, the United States is in the driver's seat. We need to make sure that in trying to solve one problem—our dependence on imported oil—we do not create a far more serious one: chaos in the world food economy.

5

Support of Biofuels Production Does Not Increase Food Insecurity

Mike Wilson

Mike Wilson, who grew up on a grain and livestock farm and studied agricultural journalism at the University of Illinois, served as editor of Prairie Farmer *and is currently executive editor of* Farm Futures.

Instead of praising America's corn farmers for meeting the rising demand for corn, the mainstream media instead blames them and the biofuels industry for rising food prices. However, rising oil prices, not the price of corn, are the cause. The cost of transporting food contributes more to food costs than commodity prices. Indeed, oil companies have a vested interest in shifting the blame to corn producers, as oil companies feel threatened by alternative fuels. Nor should the media blame the price of corn for reductions in food aid, as transportation costs also play a significant role. Rather than blame corn producers, policymakers should reform the inefficient farm bill and pass the savings on to people who need aid most.

These should be giddy days for America's corn farmers. In years past you were proud to supply the country and the world with food. And this year [2008] American farmers once again answered the call, having just harvested a record crop in both yield and acreage. The market asked for more corn and you provided it.

But instead of celebrating your accomplishments, it appears you should be ducking for cover. With food prices rising steadily this past year, the mainstream media has decided to blame biofuels—and apparently the people who grow the raw product for them—for rising food prices, even malnutrition in developing countries.

Major articles appeared late last year [2007] in major news media. CNBC's Becky Quick proclaimed, "The ethanol production push has raised demand for corn and pushed up food prices across the country without contributing much relief for gas hungry drivers, so why do we continue converting food to energy?"

The United Nation's Jean Ziegler claimed biofuels are "a crime against humanity" and should be banned for five years. Dennis Avery, Director for the Center for Global Food Issues, apocalyptically proclaimed, "We're burning food," as he shilled for more nuclear plants on CBNC. My how the spin is humming these days!

Comments like these seem comparable to shouting fire in a crowded theatre. A documentary, "King Corn," tracks the crop from planting to consumption and concludes it is to blame for all sorts of ills, including obesity. After all, don't we put corn sweetener into sodas and fatten cattle that are turned into fast food hamburgers? Apparently there is no discussion of demand for those products and the fact that someone must actually want them and pay for them before consuming them.

Sizzle sells, even when the sizzle makes no sense.

Rising Food Prices

Rising food prices appear to be the main objection now in the food vs. fuel debate. So let's get some facts into the discussion. Despite what you hear, good healthy food is still cheaper here than anywhere else on the planet. Ethanol growth will have no impact on the availability of food in U.S. grocery stores. And we proved last year [2007] we were able to grow more food crops to go into energy without dramatically increasing domestic prices.

According to the Department of Labor's Consumer Price Index, food and beverage prices were up 4.4% over a year earlier as of Oct. 2007. Both transportation and medical inflation were higher. Energy? Up a whopping 14.5%. In the first ten months of 2007 petroleum-based energy costs increased at a 20.6% annual rate. Rising oil prices, not commodity prices, are the biggest cause for food inflation. Historically, energy increases the price of food more than a commodity price.

> [G]ood healthy food is still cheaper here [in the US] than anywhere else on the planet.

Those facts may lead one to conclude the pundits are lashing out at the wrong industry. The oil companies still have a monopolistic hold on transportation fuel in this country. In 2007 revenue for Exxon Mobil Corp., the world's biggest publicly traded oil company, hit $102 billion. That is enough money to buy the entire U.S. corn production—twice over. Who is really in charge here?

Increased competition in transportation fuels will help discipline a market dominated by a handful of multinational oil companies that are extracting monopoly profits from U.S. gasoline consumers.

A Smear Campaign

In fact those who smear corn ethanol and biofuels in general have a vested interest in lower biofuel production and, secondarily, lower corn prices.

Not happy enough with record quarterly profits, oil companies are threatened by the Renewable Fuels Standard (RFS), a federal policy that mandates more and more use of biofuel blended into gasoline to reduce energy dependence on foreign sources. RFS started with 4 billion gallons in calendar year 2006 and will nearly double to 7.5 billion gallons by 2012. But America's ethanol industry is at 7.5 billion gallons now. That is why Senators like John Thune, R-S.D., have brought up an amendment in the Farm Bill that would require an RFS of 8.5 billion gallons by year-end 2008 and 36 billion gallons by 2022.

House and Senate leaders are reportedly discussing alternative language that would result in a bill requiring 20.5 billion gallons of renewable fuels by 2015, with 15 billion gallons produced from grains and 5.5 billion gallons of advanced (cellulosic) biofuels.

That higher RFS would take more market share from Big Oil, a story you probably won't hear from [television news personality] Katie Couric. You can bet that oil lobbyists are pressing the flesh on Capitol Hill and in editorial offices of the mainstream media. Their message has nothing to do with windfall profits they're making on $95 per barrel oil. It's not even how food prices are going up domestically—that might bring more attention to those higher energy prices.

No, the message is, "look what these biofuels are doing to the poor and starving of this world. We can't keep doing this." It's big on emotion, short on reality.

The other party interested in lower corn prices? Our friends in the U.S. livestock industry. My, what strange bedfellows these two make.

That's a toughie, because cattlemen are corn farmers' best customers. But National Cattlemen's Beef Association (NCBA) policy is specifically opposed to increasing the government mandate. "For cattlemen, any increase to the RFS mandate would be too much because renewable fuels production should be market driven, not government driven," says Jason Jordan, NCBA manager of legislative affairs.

"Subsidized ethanol production and mandated demand through an inflated RFS—when the infrastructure is just now developing—is a recipe for disaster when there's a short corn crop," adds NCBA Chief Economist Gregg Doud.

But the fact that biofuel infrastructure is still developing is a good case for growing the RFS. Ethanol plants may or may not break even this year without more demand, even if it is from mandates. Those plants will be mothballed.

Food Aid Drops

Higher commodity prices are getting blamed for a recent sharp drop in food aid. According to World Food Program, (WFP), a UN-funded humanitarian organization, aid has dropped from 10 million tons in 1995 to 6.7 million tons last year—the lowest in 15 years and 18% lower than in 2005.

True, demand for our commodities has driven world prices higher. But that demand has almost zero impact on African farmers, or subsistence farmers in general, because subsistence farmers don't compete in that world commodity market. Whether our corn is $2 or $4 probably makes no difference to them.

Where the argument is correct is how higher prices—both oil and commodities—cut into budgets for groups helping to feed malnourished people.

Whether our corn is $2 or $4 probably makes no difference to [subsistence farmers].

According to John Powell, Deputy Executive Director at WFP, "The cost of obtaining basic food commodities—wheat, rice, corn—went up by some 50% over the past five years, while fuel prices have risen by an average of 40%."

Powell rightly uses the words "cost of obtaining basic food" and links that cost with the rise in energy prices.

WFP's new budget projects another increase of 35% in commodity prices over the next two years—which Powell estimates will translate into roughly 780,000 less metric tons of food it can purchase for the poor.

Higher commodity prices are a fact and we shouldn't be ashamed to profit. We'll need these higher prices as farmers get slammed with input prices jumping 20 to 30% in 2008.

A Four-Step Solution

So how do we solve the food aid situation?

- Reform the farm bill. For too long our farm policy has put money in the hands of the wrong people. Yes, only a few, but when celebrities and sports heroes are getting farm payments, the system must be reformed. If we don't reform farm policy we risk losing credibility with Joe Consumer, who may stop supporting farmers when Congress suggests we increase biofuel mandates. Plus, a more efficient farm bill could pass savings on to feed more poor people.

- Increase food aid contributions through the government program P.L. 480, the largest program available to send U.S. ag commodities to developing countries.

- Drop the mandate that says at least 75% of the gross tonnage of commodities exported under P.L. 480 must be shipped on privately owned U.S. flag commercial vessels. Open competition reduces costs and improves efficiencies.

- Start making cash contributions to developing country governments so they can make local purchases. There's a good argument for this. Providing commodities is significant and should continue, but adding cash that can then be used for local purchases boosts demand for local subsistence farmers.

This country has set a goal to wean itself off petroleum. No one said that process would be simple, easy, or less expensive. But it still remains the nation's goal.

Biofuels are not a perfect answer to the problem. They are only one piece of the puzzle. But to dismiss their potential impact on foreign oil dependence is short-sighted at best. There is no more cheap petroleum in the world. American consumers need to wake up and realize the goal to move beyond oil is attainable, but not without a change in attitude and yes, some sacrifice.

In any case, the discussion deserves thoughtful commentary, not empty rhetoric.

6

Climate Change Will Increase Food Insecurity

CARE

CARE is a non-governmental humanitarian organization that fights global poverty through relief and development, promoting self-sufficiency and the empowerment of women in developing nations. CARE also provides relief in the event of natural disasters.

The number of people facing food insecurity is growing. While several factors contribute to food insecurity, climate change will be a major driver. Indeed, research indicates that climate change will decrease global grain production 1–7 percent by 2060. Reduced grain production leads to higher food prices, which will increase hunger among the world's poorest people. Nations in which climate has a significant impact on agricultural production, such as those that depend on rain-fed grains, will feel the greatest impact. The impact on socially excluded groups such as female-headed households will be even greater. Therefore, in addition to improving agricultural practices and sustainable land-use management, climate change and food insecurity policies should also improve local governance and promote gender equality.

Food insecurity is a growing concern throughout the developing world, particularly for poor women and children. Estimates suggest that in 2010, approximately 925 million individuals were undernourished. While there have been some

CARE, "Adaptation and Food Security," *CARE International Climate Change Brief*, April 2011, pp. 1–5. All rights reserved. Reproduced with permission.

gains in reducing hunger globally, it remains a critical challenge, and it is unlikely that the Millennium Development Goal (MDG) to halve the proportion of people suffering from hunger by 2015 will be met.

A recent study on the future of food and farming identified six key drivers of change affecting the global food system: a growing global population; changing diets, notably an increase in demand for resource-intensive meat products; food system governance, including globalisation of markets, subsidies and trade restrictions; competition for resources, particularly land, water and energy; consumer values and ethics; and the impacts of climate change. The combined effects of these pressures mean that increasing numbers of people will be at risk of hunger in the coming years.

While recognising that all of these drivers represent significant factors in achieving food security for all, this [excerpt] . . . is focused on the impacts of climate change on food security in developing countries. Tackling this crisis will require unprecedented efforts on the part of the humanitarian and development community, researchers, governments, private sector and civil society organisations and farmers around the world. This brief outlines CARE's understanding of the challenge and our response.

Defining Food Security

[According to the Food and Agriculture Organization of the United Nations:] 'Food security exists when all people at all times have physical or economic access to sufficient, safe and nutritious food to meet their dietary needs and food preferences for an active and healthy life.' Food security is influenced by four key dimensions: availability of sufficient food; economic, physical and social access to the resources needed to acquire food; stability of this availability and access; and utilisation, including nutrition, food safety and quality.

Achieving food security for all requires a coordinated effort that incorporates preventive, promotional, protective and transformative measures. Preventive measures aim to help people avoid food insecurity, and include social insurance systems such as savings groups, as well as risk management measures such as crop diversification. Promotional measures aim to reduce vulnerability to food insecurity by enhancing incomes and capacities, for example through microcredit schemes. Protective actions are relief measures, required when preventive and promotional measures fail. Underpinning these three types of action are transformative measures that seek to address issues of social inequity and exclusion.

[W]ithout significant reductions in greenhouse gas emissions, climate change 'will greatly increase hunger, especially in the poorest parts of the world.'

Climate Change Impacts on Food Security

It is estimated that food production will need to increase by 50 percent by 2030 just to keep up with the demands of a growing global population. At the same time, climate change is projected to cause decreases in global cereal production of 1–7 percent by 2060, depending on the climate model used for the projection. These decreases will be greatest in developing countries, and particularly in South Asia and sub-Saharan Africa. Reduced production leads to higher food prices and increasing food insecurity, particularly for rural families in developing countries who are net buyers of food.

A recent study by the World Food Programme (WFP) found that without significant reductions in greenhouse gas emissions, climate change 'will greatly increase hunger, especially in the poorest parts of the world'. Assuming that current trends in population growth and inequitable distribution of wealth are maintained, WFP estimate that globally, 10–20 percent more people will be at risk of hunger by 2050 than would be without climate change. Of these, almost all will be in developing countries, with 65 percent expected to be in Africa. This has severe implications for nutrition, particularly for children. In sub-Saharan Africa, it is estimated that 10 million more children will be malnourished as a result of climate change.

The risk of hunger resulting from climate change is the result of both direct impacts on food systems, and of indirect impacts that affect the different dimensions of food security. . . . The interactions between the climate and the food system are complex and vary greatly based on local circumstances. Therefore, both the climate change impacts and their consequences need to be analysed at the local level in order to plan appropriate interventions. In turn, the direct effects . . . have indirect consequences for all four dimensions of food security: availability, access, utilisation and stability. . . .

Differential Vulnerability

Vulnerability to climate change, and resultant food insecurity, is a function of exposure to climate hazards, sensitivity to climate-related shocks and stresses and capacity to adapt. The level of exposure to climate-related hazards is often determined by geography. For example, communities in coastal areas experience much higher exposure to sea level rise and related effects such as salinisation of groundwater than communities further inland. Sensitivity is often determined by livelihoods strategies, with households dependent on rain-fed agriculture, pastoralism, fisheries or other natural resource-based livelihood strategies representing particularly vulnerable groups.

People's ability to maintain food security in the face of climate change will depend significantly on their adaptive capacity. Adaptive capacity is significantly influenced by access to and control over critical resources, such as information and knowledge on climate change, natural resources such as land and water for agriculture, and opportunities for earning sustainable income.

[S]ocially excluded groups ... are highly vulnerable to the impacts of climate change and other stressors that lead to food insecurity.

Structural and relational factors such as inequitable policies, power relationships and cultural norms also play an important role in determining adaptive capacity. This means that socially excluded groups, including female-headed households, orphans, persons living with HIV&AIDS and landless people, are highly vulnerable to the impacts of climate change and other stressors that lead to food insecurity.

In many contexts, women may face higher risks of food insecurity due to gender inequality. They play a critical role in agriculture and in managing household food supplies, but may lack access to services and control over important resources and decisions affecting food security. As a result, they may become trapped in a vicious cycle, with food insecurity and malnutrition making them more vulnerable to climate change, and climate change exacerbating the risk of food insecurity. CARE is particularly focused on promoting gender equality, and in particular, on empowering women to build the resilience of their families and communities to adapt to climate change and achieve food security.

Mutually Supportive Approaches

CARE is committed to both food security and climate change adaptation as programming and policy advocacy priorities. We consider food security to be a basic human right and a critical element of household livelihood security, resilience, nutritional status and overall wellbeing. Our approach to food security focuses on empowering poor women and girls to realise food and nutrition security. It addresses all four dimensions of food security, including protecting and promoting resilient livelihoods to ensure adequate food availability and access; improving utilisation with a focus on nutritional status; and enhancing stability through vulnerability and risk reduction and management. Gender inequality, poor governance and climate change are recognized as drivers of food insecurity and malnutrition.

Therefore, our food security approach incorporates transformative activities that emphasise equity, women's empowerment, rights and appropriate governance. Promoting environmental sustainability and enhancing adaptive capacity are key elements of the approach.

Climate change is a study in injustice, as the people least responsible suffer the brunt of its impacts. CARE's approach to adaptation is focused on increasing the capacity of people, particularly the most vulnerable groups, to adapt to climate change. This includes support for climate-resilient livelihoods; disaster risk reduction; and empowerment, advocacy and social mobilisation to address the underlying causes of vulnerability, including poor governance, gender inequality and inequitable access to resources and services.

Our approaches to climate change adaptation and to food security share objectives of empowering socially excluded groups to reduce their vulnerability and increase their resilience. Our work on adaptation necessarily addresses food security as a key challenge facing climate-vulnerable populations, while our food security programming will in many cases contribute to people's capacity to adapt to climate change, particularly when climate change is explicitly taken into consideration in the design of programmes. They are mutually supportive approaches. In places where people are vulnerable to both climate change impacts and food insecurity, we are increasingly, adopting an integrated approach which addresses resilient livelihoods, risk reduction and the underlying causes of vulnerability and food insecurity.

7

Global Warming Will Not Increase Food Insecurity

Patrick J. Michaels

Patrick J. Michaels, global warming skeptic, is a fellow at the CATO institute, a free-market think tank, and author of Climate of Extremes: Global Warming Science They Don't Want You to Know.

Despite claims that global warming will lead to food shortages, in truth global warming has increased agricultural production. Because weather impacts agriculture, farmers have developed plants and technologies to resist weather shocks. As a result, global grain production has consistently increased. Policies that address global warming, not global warming itself, are responsible for rising food prices. The diversion of grain to biofuels has increased the price of food, which in turn has led to loss of life in the developing world. Ill-advised global warming policies, not global warming, threaten food security.

Almost every major American daily newspaper picked up an article published earlier this month [June 2011] by *New York Times* scribe Justin Gillis entitled "A Warming Planet Struggles to Feed Itself."

How many times have we read, in the last 50 years, that this or that environmental apocalypse is going to starve the world? I got my doctorate on the wings of one; at that time it was called "global cooling," after a 1974 CIA [Central Intelligence Agency] report leaked to the *Times* said that rapidly cooling planetary temperatures could usher in an era of heightened global instability caused by food shortages.

In my lifetime there have been a large number of predicted nutritional apocalypses, caused by overpopulation, lack of biological diversity in our food supply, genetic engineering run amok, acid rain, too little ozone, too much ozone and, finally, global warming. If there were futures on the end of the world, I'd go short. The wrong bet won't matter anyway.

Checking the Facts

Facts: Global surface temperature rose about three-fourths of a degree Celsius in the 20th century. U.S. corn yields *quintupled*. Life expectancy *doubled*. People got fat. Global warming didn't cause all of this, but increased atmospheric carbon dioxide directly stimulated plant growth. Further, greenhouse warming takes place more in the winter, which lengthens growing seasons. With adequate water, plants then fix and yield more carbohydrate.

While doing my dissertation I learned a few things about world crops. Serial adoption of new technologies produces a nearly constant increase in yields. Greater fertilizer application, improved response to fertilizer, better tractor technology, better tillage practices, old-fashioned genetic selection, and new-fashioned genetic engineering all conspire to raise yields, year after year.

Weather and climate have something to do with yields, too. Seasonal rainfall can vary a lot from year-to-year. That's "weather." If dry years become dry decades (that's "climate") farmers will switch from corn to grain sorghum, or, where possible, wheat. Breeders and scientists will continue to develop more water-efficient plants and agricultural technologies, such as no-till production.

Adaptation even applies to the home garden. The tomato variety "heat wave" sets fruit at higher temperatures than traditional cultivars.

However, Gillis claims that "[t]he rapid growth in farm output that defined the late 20th century has slowed" because of global warming.

His own figures show this is wrong. The increasing trend in world crop yields from 1960 to 1980 is exactly the same as from 1980 to 2010. And per capita grain production is rising, not falling.

Ethanol's Contribution to the Problem

Gillis more rightly could have blamed any loss in per capita consumption on the stupid (I choose my words carefully) global warming policy that greens once touted: ethanol production from corn.

Even Al Gore now admits that corn-based ethanol produces more carbon dioxide than it saves. But as a result of recent ethanol policy, we are the first nation in world history to burn up its food supply to please a political faction.

Indur Goklany, a much-published scholar on the consequences of global warming policies, recently calculated that in 2010 alone, diversion of grain to biofuels (like ethanol) caused nearly 200,000 excess deaths in the developing world because of increased prices.

Per capita grain production is going up, and stupid policies—not global warming—are putting people's food security at risk.

Roger Pielke, Jr., another noteworthy student of global warming science and policy, concurs. Regarding Gillis' piece, he says: "The carbon dioxide-centric focus on the article provides a nice illustration of how an obsession with 'global warming' can serve to distract attention from factors that actually matter more for issues of human and environmental concern."

Ever since people noticed how robust the increase of crop yields is, others have been saying that it must soon stop. This "limits to growth" argument is as tired as a farmer at the end of harvest. Two weeks ago, it was announced at the Global Wheat Rust Symposium that scientists are now producing "super varieties" of pathogen-resistant grain, which will tack another 15% onto yield. As the new strain is adopted, it will continue the linear upward trend in wheat yield for at least another decade.

I continue to be amazed at how little the facts are checked on global warming, even when writing for the so-called newspapers of record. Crop yields have increased at a constant rate despite changes in global temperature. Per capita grain production is going up, and stupid policies—not global warming—are putting people's food security at risk.

8

Overpopulation Is the Primary Cause of Food Insecurity

David Attenborough

David Attenborough, a British broadcaster and naturalist, is best known for writing and presenting the British Broadcasting Corporation's Life *series, a comprehensive survey of all life on the planet.*

Despite efforts by conservationists to protect wildlife and the environment from detrimental human activities, the threats seem to be increasing. In truth, the disasters that threaten the natural world have one root cause—the growing world population. Nevertheless, when scientists and policymakers discuss how to reduce food insecurity and slow climate change, they are silent on the issue of population control. Clearly, the resources of the earth are finite and feeding its ever-burgeoning human population will only become more difficult as the numbers grow. Since no alternatives can reduce the impact of indefinite growth, governments must develop population reduction policies and make contraception and reproductive health services freely available to all.

Fifty years ago, on 29 April 1961, a group of far-sighted people in this country [England] got together to warn the world of an impending disaster. Among them were a distin-

David Attenborough, "This Heaving Planet: Half a Century Ago, the WWF Was Formed to Help Save Endangered Animals. Today, It's Human Beings Who Are Increasingly at Risk, Through Overpopulation and Food Scarcity. Someone Needs to Say the Unsayable," *New Statesman (1996),* vol. 140, no. 5050, April 25, 2011. All rights reserved. Reproduced with permission.

guished scientist, Sir Julian Huxley; a bird-loving painter, Peter Scott; an advertising executive, Guy Mountford; a powerful and astonishingly effective civil servant, Max Nicholson—and several others.

They were all, in addition to their individual professions, dedicated naturalists, fascinated by the natural world not just in this country [England] but internationally. And they noticed what few others had done—that all over the world, charismatic animals that were once numerous were beginning to disappear.

The Arabian oryx, which once had been widespread all over the Arabian Peninsula, had been reduced to a few hundred. In Spain, there were only about 90 imperial eagles left. The Californian condor was down to about 60. In Hawaii, a goose that once lived in flocks on the lava fields around the great volcanoes had been reduced to 50. And the strange rhinoceros that lived in the dwindling forests of Java—to about 40. These were the most extreme examples. Wherever naturalists looked they found species of animals whose populations were falling rapidly. This planet was in danger of losing a significant number of its inhabitants, both animals and plants.

Something had to be done. And that group determined to do it. They would need scientific advice to discover the causes of these impending disasters and to devise ways of slowing them and, they hoped, of stopping them. They would have to raise awareness and understanding of people everywhere; and, like all such enterprises, they would need money to enable them to take practical action.

The World Wildlife Fund

They set about raising all three. Since the problem was an international one, they based themselves not in Britain but in the heart of Europe, in Switzerland. They called the organisation that they created the World Wildlife Fund (WWF).

As well as the international committee, separate action groups would be needed in individual countries. A few months after that inaugural meeting in Switzerland, Britain established one—and was the first country to do so.

The methods the WWF used to save these endangered species were several. Some, such as the Hawaiian goose and the oryx, were taken into captivity in zoos, bred up into a significant population and then taken back to their original home and released.

[T]he disasters that continue increasingly to afflict the natural world have one element that connects them all— the unprecedented increase in the number of human beings on the planet.

Elsewhere—in Africa, for example—great areas of unspoiled country were set aside as national parks, where the animals could be protected from poachers and encroaching human settlement. In the Galápagos Islands and in the home of the mountain gorillas in Rwanda, ways were found of ensuring that local people who also had claims on the land where such animals lived were able to benefit financially by attracting visitors.

Ecotourism was born. The movement as a whole went from strength to strength. Twenty four countries established their own WWF national appeals. Existing conservation bodies, of which there were a number in many parts of the world but which had been working largely in isolation, acquired new zest and international links. New ones were founded focusing on particular areas or particular species. The world awoke to conservation. Millions—billions—of dollars were raised. And now, 50 years on, conservationists who have worked so hard and with such foresight can justifiably congratulate themselves on having responded magnificently to the challenge.

Yet now, in spite of a great number of individual successes, the problem seems bigger than ever. True, thanks to the vigour and wisdom of conservationists, no major charismatic species has yet disappeared. Many are still trembling on the brink, but they are still hanging on. Today, however, overall there are more problems not fewer, more species at risk of extinction than ever before. Why?

A Growing Population

Fifty years ago, when the WWF was founded, there were about three billion people on earth. Now there are almost seven billion—over twice as many—every one of them needing space. Space for their homes, space to grow their food (or to get others to grow it for them), space to build schools, roads and airfields. Where could that come from? A little might be taken from land occupied by other people but most of it could only come from the land which, for millions of years, animals and plants had had to themselves—the natural world.

But the impact of these extra billions of people has spread even beyond the space they physically claimed. The spread of industrialisation has changed the chemical constituents of the atmosphere. The oceans that cover most of the surface of the planet have been polluted and increasingly acidified. The earth is warming. We now realise that the disasters that continue increasingly to afflict the natural world have one element that connects them all—the unprecedented increase in the number of human beings on the planet.

There have been prophets who have warned us of this impending disaster. One of the first was Thomas Malthus. His surname—Malthus—leads some to suppose that he was some continental European philosopher, a German perhaps. But he was not. He was an Englishman, born in Guildford, Surrey, in the middle of the 18th century. His most important book, *An Essay on the Principle of Population*, was published in 1798. In it, he argued that the human population would increase inexorably until it was halted by what he termed "misery and vice". Today, for some reason, that prophecy seems to be largely ignored—or, at any rate, disregarded. It is true that he did not foresee the so-called Green Revolution (from the 1940s to the late 1970s), which greatly increased the amount of food that can be produced in any given area of arable land. And there may be other advances in our food producing skills that we ourselves still cannot foresee. But such advances only delay things. The fundamental truth that Malthus proclaimed remains the truth: there cannot be more people on this earth than can be fed.

Many people would like to deny that this is so. They would like to believe in that oxymoron "sustainable growth". Kenneth Boulding, President Kennedy's environmental adviser 45 years ago, said something about this: "Anyone who believes in indefinite growth in anything physical, on a physically finite planet, is either mad—or an economist".

The population of the world is now growing by nearly 80 million a year. One and a half million a week. A quarter of a million a day. Ten thousand an hour. In this country [England] it is projected to grow by 10 million in the next 22 years. That is equivalent to ten more Birminghams.

> The fundamental truth that [Thomas] Malthus proclaimed remains the truth: there cannot be more people on this earth than can be fed.

A Perfect Storm

All these people, in [England] and worldwide, rich or poor, need and deserve food, water, energy and space. Will they be able to get it? I don't know. I hope so. But the [British] government's chief scientist and the last president of the Royal Society have both referred to the approaching "perfect storm" of population growth, climate change and peak oil production, leading inexorably to more and more insecurity in the supply of food, water and energy.

Consider food. For animals, hunger is a regular feature of their lives. The stoical desperation of the cheetah cubs whose mother failed in her last few attempts to kill prey for them, and who consequently face starvation, is very touching. But that happens to human beings, too. All of us who have travelled in poor countries have met people for whom hunger is a daily background ache in their lives. There are about a billion such people today—that is four times as many as the entire human population of this planet a mere 2,000 years ago, at the time of Christ.

[T]he approaching 'perfect storm' of population growth, climate change and peak oil production, [lead] inexorably to more and more insecurity in the supply of food, water and energy.

You may be aware of the government's Foresight project, Global Food and Farming Futures. It shows how hard it is to feed the seven billion of us alive today. It lists the many obstacles that are already making this harder to achieve—soil erosion, salinisation, the depletion of aquifers, over-grazing, the spread of plant diseases as a result of globalisation, the absurd growing of food crops to turn into biofuels to feed motor cars instead of people—and so on. So it underlines how desperately difficult it is going to be to feed a population that is projected to stabilise "in the range of eight to ten billion people by the year 2050". It recommends the widest possible range of measures across all disciplines to tackle this. And it makes a number of eminently sensible recommendations, including a second green revolution.

But, surprisingly, there are some things that the project report does not say. It doesn't state the obvious fact that it would be much easier to feed eight billion people than ten billion. Nor does it suggest that the measures to achieve such a number—such as family planning and the education and empowerment of women—should be a central part of any programme that aims to secure an adequate food supply for humanity. It doesn't refer to the prescient statement 40 years ago by Norman Borlaug, the Nobel laureate and father of the first green revolution.

[E]very mother subsisting on the equivalent of a dollar a day already knows—that her children would be better fed if there were four of them around the table instead of ten.

Borlaug produced new strains of high-yielding, short-strawed and disease-resistant wheat and in doing so saved many thousands of people in India, Pakistan, Africa and Mexico from starvation. But he warned us that all he had done was to give us a "breathing space" in which to stabilise our numbers. The government's report anticipates that food prices may rise with oil prices, and makes it clear that this will affect poorest people worst and discusses various way to help them. But it doesn't mention what every mother subsisting on the equivalent of a dollar a day already knows—that her children would be better fed if there were four of them around the table instead of ten. These are strange omissions.

How can we ignore the chilling statistics on arable land? In 1960 there was more than one acre of good cropland per person in the world—enough to sustain a reasonable European diet. Today, there is only half an acre each. In China, it is only a quarter of an acre, because of their dramatic problems of soil degradation.

A Strange Silence

Another impressive government report on biodiversity published this year, *Making Space for Nature in a Changing World*, is rather similar. It discusses all the rising pressures on wildlife in the UK—but it doesn't mention our growing population as being one of them—which is particularly odd when you consider that England is already the most densely populated country in Europe.

Most bizarre of all was a recent report by a royal commission on the environmental impact of demographic change in this country [England] which denied that population size was a problem at all—as though 10 million extra people, more or less, would have no real impact. Of course it is not our only or even our main environmental problem but it is absurd to deny that, as a multiplier of all the others, it is a problem.

I suspect that you could read a score of reports by bodies concerned with global problems—and see that population is one of the drivers that underlies all of them—and yet find no reference to this obvious fact in any of them. Climate change tops the environmental agenda at present. We all know that every additional person will need to use some carbon energy, if only firewood for cooking, and will therefore create more carbon dioxide—though a rich person will produce vastly more than a poor one. Similarly, we can all see that every extra person is—or will be—an extra victim of climate change—though the poor will undoubtedly suffer more than the rich. Yet not a word of it appeared in the voluminous documents emerging from the [2009] Copenhagen and [2010] Cancún climate summits.

Why this strange silence? I meet no one who privately disagrees that population growth is a problem. No one—except flat-earthers—can deny that the planet is finite. We can all see it—in that beautiful picture of our earth taken by the Apollo mission. So why does hardly anyone say so publicly? There seems to be some bizarre taboo around the subject.

The Population Control Taboo

This taboo doesn't just inhibit politicians and civil servants who attend the big conferences. It even affects the environmental and developmental non-governmental organisations

[NGOs], the people who claim to care most passionately about a sustainable and prosperous future for our children.

Yet their silence implies that their admirable goals can be achieved regardless of how many people there are in the world or the UK, even though they all know that they can't.

The sooner we stabilise our numbers, the sooner we stop running up the 'down' escalator.

I simply don't understand it. It is all getting too serious for such fastidious niceties. It remains an obvious and brutal fact that on a finite planet human population will quite definitely stop at some point. And that can only happen in one of two ways. It can happen sooner, by fewer human births—in a word, by contraception. That is the humane way, the powerful option that allows all of us to deal with the problem, if we collectively choose to do so. The alternative is an increased death rate—the way that all other creatures must suffer, through famine or disease or predation. That, translated into human terms, means famine or disease or war—over oil or water or food or minerals or grazing rights or just living space. There is, alas, no third alternative of indefinite growth.

The sooner we stabilise our numbers, the sooner we stop running up the "down" escalator. Stop population increase—stop the escalator—and we have some chance of reaching the top; that is to say, a decent life for all.

To do that requires several things. First and foremost, it needs a much wider understanding of the problem, and that will not happen while the taboo on discussing it retains such a powerful grip on the minds of so many worthy and intelligent people. Then it needs a change in our culture so that while everyone retains the right to have as many children as they like, they understand that having large families means compounding the problems their children and everyone else's children will face in the future.

A Need for Action

It needs action by governments. In my view, all countries should develop a population policy—as many as 70 countries already have them in one form or another—and give it priority. The essential common factor is to make family planning and other reproductive health services freely available to every one, and empower and encourage them to use it—though without any kind of coercion.

According to the Global Footprint Network, there are already more than a hundred countries whose combination of numbers and affluence have already pushed them past the sustainable level. They include almost all developed countries. The UK is one of the worst. There the aim should be to reduce over time both the consumption of natural resources per person and the number of people—while, needless to say, using the best technology to help maintain living standards. It is tragic that the only current population policies in developed countries are, perversely, attempting to increase their birth rates in order to look after the growing number of old people. The notion of ever more old people needing ever more young people, who will in turn grow old and need even more young people, and so on ad infinitum, is an obvious ecological Ponzi scheme.

I am not an economist, nor a sociologist, nor a politician, and it is from their disciplines that answers must come. But I am a naturalist. Being one means that I know something of the factors that keep populations of different species of animals within bounds and what happens when they aren't.

I am aware that every pair of blue tits nesting in my garden is able to lay over 20 eggs a year but, as a result of predation or lack of food, only one or two will, at best, survive. I have watched lions ravage the hundreds of wildebeest fawns that are born each year on the plains of Africa.

I have seen how increasing numbers of elephants can devastate their environment until, one year when the rains fail on the already over-grazed land, they die in hundreds. But we are human beings. Because of our intelligence, and our ever-increasing skills and sophisticated technologies, we can avoid such brutalities. We have medicines that prevent our children from dying of disease. We have developed ways of growing increasing amounts of food. But we have removed the limiters that keep animal populations in check. So now our destiny is in our hands.

There is one glimmer of hope. Wherever women have the vote, wherever they are literate and have the medical facilities to control the number of children they bear, the birth rate falls. All those civilised conditions exist in the southern Indian state of Kerala. In India as a whole, the total fertility rate is 2.8 births per woman. In Kerala, it is 1.7 births per woman. In Thailand last year, it was 1.8 per woman, similar to that in Kerala. But compare that with the mainly Catholic Philippines, where it is 3.3.

Breaking the Taboo

Here and there, at last, there are signs of a recognition of the problem. Save the Children mentioned it in its last report. The Royal Society has assembled a working party of scientists across a wide range of disciplines who are examining the problem.

But what can each of us do? Well, there is just one thing that I would ask. Break the taboo, in private and in public—as best you can, as you judge right. Until it is broken there is no hope of the action we need. Wherever and whenever we speak of the environment, we should add a few words to ensure that the population element is not ignored. If you are a member of a relevant NGO, invite them to acknowledge it.

If you belong to a church—and especially if you are a Catholic, because its doctrine on contraception is a major factor in this problem—suggest they consider the ethical issues involved. I see the Anglican bishops in Australia have dared to do so. If you have contacts in government, ask why the growth of our population, which affects every department, is as yet no one's responsibility. Big empty Australia has appointed a sustainable population minister, so why can't small crowded Britain?

The Hawaiian goose, the oryx, and the imperial eagle that sounded the environmental alarm 50 years ago were, you might say, the equivalent of canaries in coal mines—warnings of impending and even wider catastrophe.

Make a list of all the other environmental problems that now afflict us and our poor battered planet—the increase of greenhouse gases and consequential global warming, the acidification of the oceans and the collapse of fish stocks, the loss of rainforest, the spread of deserts, the shortage of arable land, the increase in violent weather, the growth of megacities, famine, migration patterns. The list goes on and on. But they all share one underlying cause. Every one of these global problems, social as well as environmental, becomes more difficult—and ultimately impossible—to solve with ever more people.

9

Modernization and Global Trade Will Reduce Food Insecurity

Robert Paarlberg

Robert Paarlberg, professor of political science at Wellesley College and an associate at Harvard University's Weatherhead Center for International Affairs, is author of Food Politics: What Everyone Needs to Know.

Buying organic food that is grown locally, using slow, outdated farming practices will not reduce hunger for the world's poor. In fact, low farming productivity contributes to the poverty that leads to hunger. Indeed, foreign aid policies that oppose agricultural modernization increase food insecurity. To help reduce hunger, policymakers should abandon the romantic notion that pre-industrial food and farming techniques are better. During the Green Revolution of the 1960s, foreign assistance that supported modern farming techniques, agricultural education, and improvements in road and irrigation brought India from the brink of famine. Since organic farming increases health risks and pollution, foreign aid should instead support high-tech farming techniques that help farmers increase the quantity and quality of their yields.

From Whole Foods recyclable cloth bags to Michelle Obama's organic White House garden, modern eco-foodies are full of good intentions. We want to save the planet. Help local farmers. Fight climate changed—and childhood obesity, too. But though it's certainly a good thing to be thinking about global welfare while chopping our certified organic onions, the hope that we can help others by changing our shopping and eating habits is being wildly oversold to Western consumers. Food has become an elite preoccupation in the West, ironically, just as the most effective ways to address hunger in poor countries have fallen out of fashion.

Helping the world's poor feed themselves is no longer the rallying cry it once was. Food may be today's cause célèbre, but in the pampered West, that means trendy causes like making food "sustainable"—in other words, organic, local, and slow. Appealing as that might sound, it is the wrong recipe for helping those who need it the most. Even our understanding of the global food problem is wrong these days, driven too much by the single issue of international prices. In April 2008, when the cost of rice for export had tripled in just six months and wheat reached its highest price in 28 years, a *New York Times* editorial branded this a "World Food Crisis." World Bank President Robert Zoellick warned that high food prices would be particularly damaging in poor countries, where "there is no margin for survival." Now that international rice prices are down 40 percent from their peak and wheat prices have fallen by more than half, we too quickly conclude that the crisis is over. Yet 850 million people in poor countries were chronically undernourished before the 2008 price spike, and the number is even larger now, thanks in part to last year's global recession. This is the real food crisis we face.

The Truth About Food Prices

It turns out that food prices on the world market tell us very little about global hunger. International markets for food, like most other international markets, are used most heavily by the well-to-do, who are far from hungry. The majority of truly undernourished people—62 percent, according to the U.N.

Food and Agriculture Organization—live in either Africa or South Asia, and most are small farmers or rural landless laborers living in the countryside of Africa and South Asia. They are significantly shielded from global price fluctuations both by the trade policies of their own governments and by poor roads and infrastructure. In Africa, more than 70 percent of rural households are cut off from the closest urban markets because, for instance, they live more than a 30-minute walk from the nearest all-weather road.

Poverty—caused by the low income productivity of farmers labor—is the primary source of hunger in Africa, and the problem is only getting worse. The number of "food insecure" people in Africa (those consuming less than 2,100 calories a day) will increase 30 percent over the next decade without significant reforms, to 645 million, the U.S. Agriculture Department projects.

What's so tragic about this is that we know from experience how to fix the problem. Wherever the rural poor have gained access to improved roads, modern seeds, less expensive fertilizer, electrical power, and better schools and clinics, their productivity and their income have increased. But recent efforts to deliver such essentials have been undercut by deeply misguided (if sometimes well-meaning) advocacy against agricultural modernization and foreign aid.

> *Poverty—caused by the low income productivity of farmers' labor—is the primary source of hunger in Africa. . . .*

In Europe and the United States, a new line of thinking has emerged in elite circles that opposes bringing improved seeds and fertilizers to traditional farmers and opposes linking those farmers more closely to international markets. Influential food writers, advocates, and celebrity restaurant owners are repeating the mantra that "sustainable food" in the future must be organic, local, and slow. 'But guess what; Rural Africa already has such a system, and it doesn't work. Few smallholder farmers in Africa use any synthetic chemicals, so their food is de facto organic. High transportation costs force them to purchase and sell almost all of their food locally. And food preparation is painfully slow. The result is nothing to celebrate: average income levels of only $1 a day and a one-in-three chance of being malnourished.

If we are going to get serious about solving global hunger, we need to de-romanticize our view of preindustrial food and farming. And that means learning to appreciate the modern, science-intensive, and highly capitalized agricultural system we've developed in the West. Without it, our food would be more expensive and less safe. In other words, a lot like the hunger-plagued rest of the world.

Original Sins

Thirty years ago, had someone asserted in a prominent journal or newspaper that the Green Revolution was a failure, he or she would have been quickly dismissed. Today the charge is surprisingly common. Celebrity author and eco-activist Vandana Shiva claims the Green Revolution has brought nothing to India except "indebted and discontented farmers." A 2002 meeting in Rome of 500 prominent international NGOs [nongovernmental organizations], including Friends of the Earth and Greenpeace, even blamed the Green Revolution for the rise in world hunger. Let's set the record straight.

The development and introduction of high-yielding wheat and rice seeds into poor countries, led by American scientist Norman Borlaug and others in the 1960s and 70s, paid huge dividends. In Asia these new seeds lifted tens of millions of small farmers out of desperate poverty and finally ended the threat of periodic famine. India, for instance, doubted its wheat production between 1964 and 1970 and was able to terminate all dependence on international food aid by 1975. As for indebted and discontented farmers, India's rural poverty rate fell from 60 percent to just 27 percent today. Dismissing these great achievements as a "myth" (the official view of Food First, a California-based organization that campaigns globally against agricultural modernization) is just silly.

It's true that the story of the Green Revolution is not everywhere a happy one. When powerful new farming technologies are introduced into deeply unjust rural social systems, the poor tend to lose out. In Latin America, where access to good agricultural land and credit has been narrowly controlled by traditional elites, the improved seeds made available by the Green Revolution *increased* income gaps. Absentee landlords in Central America, who previously allowed peasants to plant subsistence crops on underutilized land, pushed them off to sell or rent the land to commercial growers who could turn a profit using the new seeds. Many of the displaced rural poor became slum dwellers. Yet even in Latin America, the prevalence of hunger declined more than 50 percent between 1980 and 2005.

> *If Africa were to put greater resources into farm technology, irrigation, and rural roads, small farmers would benefit.*

In Asia, the Green Revolution seeds performed just as well on small nonmechanized farms as on larger farms. Wherever small farmers had sufficient access to credit, they took up the new technology just as quickly as big farmers, which led to dramatic income gains and no increase in inequality or social friction. Even poor landless laborers gained, because more abundant crops meant more work at harvest time, increasing rural wages. In Asia, the Green Revolution was good for both agriculture and social justice.

And Africa? Africa has a relatively equitable and secure distribution of land, making if more like Asia than Latin

America and increasing the chances that improvements in farm technology will help the poor. If Africa were to put greater resources into farm technology, irrigation, and rural roads, small farmers would benefit.

Organic Myths

There are other common objections to doing what is necessary to solve the real hunger crisis. Most revolve around caveats that purist critics raise regarding food systems in the United States and Western Europe. Yet such concerns, though well-intentioned, are often misinformed and counterproductive—especially when applied to the developing world.

Take industrial food systems, the current bugaboo of American food writers. Yes, they have many unappealing aspects, but without them food would be not only less abundant but also less safe. Traditional food systems lacking in reliable refrigeration and sanitary packaging are dangerous vectors for diseases. Surveys over the past several decades by the Centers for Disease Control and Prevention have found that the U.S. food supply became steadily safer over time, thanks in part to the introduction of industrial-scale technical improvements. Since 2000, the incidence of *E. coli* contamination in beef has fallen 45 percent. Today in the United States, most hospitalizations and fatalities from unsafe food come not from sales of contaminated products at supermarkets, but from the mishandling or improper preparation of food inside the home. Illness outbreaks from contaminated foods sold in stores still occur, but the fatalities are typically quite limited. A nationwide scare over unsafe spinach in 2006 triggered the virtual suspension of all fresh and bagged spinach sales, but only three known deaths were recorded. Incidents swell as these command attention in part because they are now so rare. Food Inc. should be criticized for filling our plates with too many foods that are unhealthy, but not foods that are unsafe.

Where industrial-scale food technologies have not yet reached into the developing world, contaminated food remains a major risk. In Africa, where many foods are still purchased in open-air markets (often uninspected, unpackaged, unlabeled, unrefrigerated, unpasteurized, and unwashed), an estimated 700,000 people die every year from food- and waterborne diseases, compared with an estimated 5,000 in the United States.

Food grown organically—that is, without any synthetic nitrogen fertilizers or pesticides—is not an answer to the health and safety issues. The *American Journal of Clinical Nutrition* last year published a study of 162 scientific papers from the past 50 years on the health benefits of organically grown foods and found no nutritional advantage over conventionally grown foods. According to the Mayo Clinic, "No conclusive evidence shows that organic food is more nutritious than is conventionally grown food."

Health professionals also reject the claim that organic food is safer to eat due to lower pesticide residues. Food and Drug Administration surveys have revealed that the highest dietary exposures to pesticide residues on foods in the United States are so trivial (less than one one-thousandth of a level that would cause toxicity) that the safety gains from buying organic are insignificant. Pesticide exposures remain a serious problem in the developing world, where farm chemical use is not as well regulated, yet even there they are more an occupational risk for unprotected farmworkers than a residue risk for food consumers.

When it comes to protecting the environment, assessments of organic farming become more complex. Excess nitrogen fertilizer use on conventional farms in the United States has polluted rivers and created a "dead zone" in the Gulf of Mexico, but halting synthetic nitrogen fertilizer use entirely (as farmers must do in the United States to get organic certification from the Agriculture Department) would cause environmental problems far worse.

Here's why: Less than 1 percent of American cropland is under certified organic production. If the other 99 percent were to switch to organic and had to fertilize crops without any synthetic nitrogen fertilizer, that would require a lot more composted animal manure. To supply enough organic fertilizer, the U.S. cattle population would have to increase roughly fivefold. And because those animals would have to be raised organically on forage crops, much of the land in the lower 48 states would need to be converted to pasture. Organic field crops also have lower yields per hectare. If Europe tried to feed itself organically, it would need an additional 28 million hectares of cropland, equal to all of the remaining forest cover in France, Germany, Britain, and Denmark combined.

Mass deforestation probably isn't what organic advocates intend. The smart way to protect against nitrogen runoff is to reduce synthetic fertilizer applications with taxes, regulations, and cuts in farm subsidies, but not try to go all the way to zero as required by the official organic standard. Scaling up registered organic farming would be on balance harmful, not helpful, to the natural environment.

The Greening of Modern Farming

Not only is organic farming less friendly to the environment than assumed, but modern conventional farming is becoming significantly more sustainable. High-tech farming in rich countries today is far safer for the environment, per bushel of production, than it was in the 1960s, when Rachel Carson criticized the indiscriminate farm use of DDT [dichlorodiphenyl-trichloroethane] in her environmental classic, *Silent Spring*. Thanks in part to Carson's devastating critique, that era's most damaging insecticides were banned and replaced by chemicals that could be applied in lower volume and were less persistent in the environment. Chemical use in American agriculture peaked soon thereafter, in 1973. This was a major victory for environmental advocacy.

And it was just the beginning of what has continued as a significant greening of modern farming in the United States. Soil erosion on farms dropped sharply in the 1970s with the introduction of "no-till" seed planting, an innovation that also reduced dependence on diesel fuel because fields no longer had to be plowed every spring. Farmers then began conserving water by moving to drip irrigation and by leveling their fields with lasers to minimize wasteful runoff. In the 1990s, GPS [global positioning satellite] equipment was added to tractors, autosteering the machines in straighter paths and telling farmers exactly where they were in the field to within one square meter, allowing precise adjustments in chemical use. Infrared sensors were brought in to detect the greenness of the crop, telling a farmer exactly how much more (or less) nitrogen might be needed as the growing season went forward. To reduce wasteful nitrogen use, equipment was developed that can insert fertilizers into the ground at exactly the depth needed and in perfect rows, only where it will be taken up by the plant roots.

These "precision farming" techniques have, significantly reduced the environmental footprint of modern agriculture relative to the quantity of food being produced. In 2008, the Organization for Economic Cooperation and Development published a review of the "environmental performance of agriculture" in the world's 30 most advanced industrial countries—those with the most highly capitalized and science-intensive farming systems. The results showed that between 1990 and 2004, food production in these countries continued to increase (by 5 percent in volume), yet adverse environmental impacts were reduced in every category. The land area taken up by farming declined 4 percent, soil erosion from both wind and water fell, gross greenhouse gas emissions from farming declined 3 percent, and excessive nitrogen fertilizer use fell 17 percent. Biodiversity also improved, as increased numbers of crop varieties and livestock breeds came into use.

Food aid doesn't help farmers become more productive— and it can create long-term dependency.

Seeding the Future

Africa faces a food crisis, but it's not because the continent's population is growing faster than its potential to produce food, as vintage Malthusians [after English scholar Thomas Malthus] such as environmental advocate Lester Brown and advocacy organizations such as Population Action International would have it. Food production in Africa is vastly less than the region's known potential, and that is why so many millions are going hungry there. African farmers still use almost no fertilizer; only 4 percent of cropland has been improved with irrigation; and most of the continent's cropped area is not planted with seeds improved through scientific plant breeding, so cereal yields are only a fraction of what they could be, Africa is failing to keep up with population growth not because it has exhausted its potential, but instead because too little has been invested in reaching that potential.

One reason for this failure has been sharply diminished assistance from international donors. When agricultural modernization went out of fashion among elites in the developed world beginning in the 1980s, development assistance to farming in poor countries collapsed. Per capita food production in Africa was declining during the 1980s and 1990s and the number of hungry people on the continent was doubling, but the U.S. response was to withdraw development assistance and simply ship more food aid to Africa. Food aid doesn't help farmers become more productive—and it can create long-term dependency. But in recent years, the dollar value of U.S. food aid to Africa has reached 20 times the dollar value of agricultural development assistance.

A Better Alternative

The alternative is right in front of us. Foreign assistance to support agricultural improvements has a strong record of success, when undertaken with purpose. In the 1960s, international assistance from the Rockefeller Foundation, the Ford Foundation, and donor governments led by the United States made Asia's original Green Revolution possible. U.S. assistance to India provided critical help in improving agricultural education, launching a successful agricultural extension service, and funding advanced degrees for Indian agricultural specialists at universities in the United States. The U.S. Agency for International Development, with the World Bank, helped finance fertilizer plants and infrastructure projects, including rural roads and irrigation. India could not have done this on its own—the country was on the brink of famine at the time and dangerously dependent on food aid. But instead of suffering a famine in 1975, as some naysayers had predicted, India that year celebrated a final and permanent end to its need for food aid.

Foreign assistance to farming has been a high-payoff investment everywhere, including Africa. The World Bank has documented average rates of return on investments in agricultural research in Africa of 35 percent a year, accompanied by significant reductions in poverty. Some research investments in African agriculture have brought rates of return estimated at 68 percent. Blind to these realities, the United States cut its assistance to agricultural research in Africa 77 percent between 1980 and 2006.

When it comes to Africa's growing hunger, governments in rich countries face a stark choice: They can decide to support a steady new infusion of financial and technical assistance to help local governments and farmers become more productive, or they can take a "worry later" approach and he forced to address hunger problems with increasingly expensive shipments of food aid. Development skeptics and farm modernization critics keep pushing us toward this unappealing second path. It's time for leaders with vision and political courage to push back.

10

Biotechnology Will Reduce Food Insecurity

V. Ravichandran

V. Ravichandran, a member of the Truth About Trade and Technology Global Farmer Network, owns a 60-acre farm near Poongulam Village in Tamil Nadu, India, where he grows rice, sugar cane, cotton, and pulses (small grains).

Biotechnology provides safer food in the quantities needed to feed the growing population. Unfortunately, advocates of outdated organic farming practices have convinced policymakers that they should oppose biotechnology until the technology is proven to cause no harm, a standard that is impossible to meet even for organic farming. For example, India must increase its food production to keep up with population growth. Nevertheless, the Indian government continues to oppose new biotech crops when biotech crops such as Bt cotton require fewer resources and produce greater yields. Policymakers should respect scientifically proven results and embrace biotech crops.

Investigators are still trying to determine the root cause of the *E. coli* outbreak in Germany, but they already know the grim death toll: 50 lives gone as of last weekend [July 2011], due to the consumption of bean sprouts contaminated by a new strain of the bacteria.

The source of fatalities may be an organic farm in Germany or possibly seeds grown in Egypt. What we know for

V. Ravichandran, "Food Security Depends on the Truth of Science," *Truth About Trade and Technology*, July 7, 2011. All rights reserved. Reproduced with permission.

certain right now is that the solution to the problem of food-borne illness is technology—and that's true whether we're talking about advanced nations in Europe or developing countries, such as my own, in Asia and Africa.

Yet many influential advocacy groups seem to think otherwise. These self-appointed guardians of our food supply fight modern farming practices like biotechnology and irradiation—approaches to agriculture that might have stopped the spread of the deadly German affliction. They would have jumped all over a health crisis that implicates genetically modified crops, for example. When the potential culprit is the primitive techniques of the organic food industry, however, they hush up and hope the unpleasantness simply will go away.

[W]hen our nation needs its farmers to produce more, we're forced to make do with less help ... biotechnology offers one way out of this dilemma.

Here in India, we may pay dearly for their silence because we desperately need access to the best agricultural methods in order to produce safe food as well as enough of it.

By some estimates, India must double its food output by 2020 just to keep up with a booming population. At the same time, we're seeing reliable farm hands flee from rural areas for improved economic opportunities in cities. So when our nation needs its farmers to produce more, we're forced to make do with less help.

Biotechnology offers one way out of this dilemma. As an Indian farmer who grows Bt cotton, I've seen its potential firsthand. I've grown biotech cotton since it was first approved for commercial cultivation in 2002. It's nothing less than a miracle crop that requires fewer resources and produces greater yields than old-fashioned cotton. Most cotton farmers agree with me: I suspect that more than 90 percent of India's cotton famers take advantage of biotechnology.

A Phony Controversy

Yet our government has refused to approve biotechnology in food crops such as brinjal (eggplant), in large part because political activists have created a phony controversy fueled by scientific ignorance.

The enemies of biotechnology are always touting the "precautionary principle," which is the European idea that innovations must be shown to be completely risk-free before the public can take advantage of them. This is a virtually impossible test to meet and it stands in the way of Indian progress in agriculture.

Applying this same standard to organic agriculture probably would wipe out the whole industry. Many Indian farmers, including a lot of organic farmers, use a traditional crop-protection tool called panchagavya. Its ingredients include cow dung and cow urine.

Indian farmers have used panchagavya for generations and I'm personally convinced that it's safe. But there's also little doubt in my mind that if European farmers were to seek permission to use panchagavya, they would have a hard time winning approval from regulators who rely on the precautionary principle.

The double-standard is maddening. Biotech crops are built to resist the pests and infections that create pathways to disease, including E. coli infections—and yet they're treated with insurmountable levels of suspicion by activist groups that claim to care about our food supply. The same is true with irradiation, a treatment that might very well have destroyed the E. coli in those German bean sprouts. In a terrible irony, the German government once blocked a European Commission proposal to make more use of irradiation, possibly even turning it into what some have called "the fourth pillar of public health," alongside the chlorination of water, the vaccination of children, and the pasteurization of milk and other liquids.

We won't ever completely eliminate diseases from our food—but we can contain them, if we're willing to embrace biotechnology and irradiation.

I'm hopeful that India will live up to its national motto: "sathyameva jayate." In Sanskrit, that means "truth alone triumphs." When it comes to food security, our obligation is to listen to the truth of science rather than the lies of scaremongers.

11

Crop Biodiversity, Not Altered Genetics, Will Reduce Food Insecurity

Janet Cotter and Reyes Tirado

Janet Cotter, an expert on terrestrial ecological systems, works with the Greenpeace International Science Unit at the University of Exeter, United Kingdom. Reyes Tirado works with Greenpeace Research Laboratories, where she helps shape the organizations Sustainable Agriculture campaign.

Climate change poses a serious threat to food security, especially in poorer countries. Indeed, extreme weather and unpredictable rainfall have a significant impact on agriculture. Research demonstrates that increasing biodiversity is the best way to reduce the impact of climate change on food security. Mixing crops and varieties increases resistance to weather changes. For example, rice using mixed breeding techniques resists the impact of flooding. On the other hand, no evidence shows that genetically engineered (GE) plants will reduce the impact of climate change. GE crops were developed to resist herbicides and insects, but during extreme weather, some farmers who used GE crops experienced severe losses.

Some of the most profound and direct impacts of climate change over the next few decades will be on agriculture and food systems. All quantitative assessments show that climate change will adversely affect food security.

The Impact of Climate Change

Increasing temperatures, declining and more unpredictable rainfall, more frequent extreme weather and higher severity of pest and disease are among the more drastic changes that would impact food production. However, global trends mask tremendous regional differences, with the poorest being most at risk both by global climate variations and global commodity price fluctuations. Some of the most important effects of global climate change will be felt among smallholder farmers, predominantly in developing countries.

The latest Intergovernmental Panel on Climate Change (IPCC) report predicts the probability of more heat waves, heavy rainfall, droughts and other extreme weather throughout the 21st century.

The biggest problem for food security will be the predicted increase in extreme weather, which will damage crops at particular developmental stages and make the timing of farming more difficult. . . .

Warming in the Indian Ocean and an increasingly "El Niño-like" climate could reduce main-season precipitation across most of Africa, East and South Asia, and Central and South America.

It has been shown that by 2080, the 40 poorest countries, located predominantly in tropical Africa and Latin America, could lose 10 to 20 percent of their basic grain growing capacity due to drought. The biggest problem for food security will be the predicted increase in extreme weather, which will damage crops at particular developmental stages and make the timing of farming more difficult, reducing farmers' incentives to cultivate.

A Natural Insurance Policy

Diversity farming is the single most important modern technology to achieve food security in a changing climate. Scientists have shown that diversity provides a natural insurance policy against major ecosystem changes, be it in the wild or in agriculture. It is now predicted that genetic diversity will be most crucial in highly variable environments and those under rapid human-induced climate change.

The larger the number of different species or varieties present in one field or in an ecosystem, the greater the probability that at least some of them can cope with changing conditions. Species diversity also reduces the probability of pests and diseases by diluting the availability of their hosts. It is an age old insurance policy of farming communities to hedge their risks and plant diverse crops or varieties. The strategy is not to maximise yield in an optimum year, but to maximise yield over years, good and bad, by decreasing the chance of crop failure in a bad year.

Diversity farming is the single most important modern technology to achieve food security in a changing climate.

The Scientific Data

This diversification strategy is backed by a wealth of recent scientific data:

- In a unique cooperation project among Chinese scientists and farmers in Yunnan during 1998 and 1999, researchers calculated the effect of diversity on the severity of rice blast, the major disease of rice. They showed that disease-susceptible rice varieties planted with resistant varieties had an 89 percent greater yield than when they were grown in a monoculture. Mixed varieties of rice produced more grain per hectare than their corresponding monocultures in all cases; close to 20 percent more land is needed in a monoculture to produce the same amount of hybrid and glutinous rice as was produced in a mixture. The experiment was so successful that fungicidal sprays were no longer applied by the end of the two-year programme. The practice expanded to more than 40,000 hectares in 2000, and now includes some varieties that were formerly locally extinct. This is especially remarkable as the yield gains were on top of already high average yields in the region, at nearly 10 tonnes per hectare; among the highest in the world. This shows that greater rice diversity means lower rates of plant disease and greater yields while conserving genetic diversity, all at minimal cost for farmers and the environment.

- Off the German coast, a genetically diverse area of seagrass was not only able to survive a heat wave, but experienced 26–34 percent more growth than seagrass monocultures, showing how genetic diversity increases the ability for plants to recover after a perturbation, while genetic monocultures have a limited short-term ability to respond to extreme climatic events.

- In Italy, a high level of genetic diversity within wheat fields on non-irrigated farms reduces risk of crop failure during dry conditions. A scenario where rainfall declines by 20 percent, the wheat yield would fall sharply, but when diversity is increased by 2 percent, this decline can not only be reversed but above average yields achieved.

- Agronomists in the United States compared corn yields between fields planted as monocultures and those with various levels of intercropping in Michigan over three years. They found the yields in fields with the highest diversity (three crops, plus three cover crops) were over

100 percent higher than in continuous monocultures. Crop diversity improved soil fertility, reducing the need to use chemical inputs while maintaining high yields.

There is abundant scientific evidence that crop biodiversity has an important role to play in the adaptation to our changing environment. While oversimplified farming systems, such as monocultures of genetically identical plants, would not be able to cope with a changing climate, increasing the biodiversity of an agro-ecosystem can help maintain its long-term productivity and contribute significantly to food security. Genetic diversity within a field provides a buffer against losses caused by environmental change, pests and diseases. Genetic diversity provides the resilience needed for a reliable and stable, long-term food production.

Increasing the biodiversity of an agro-ecosystem can help maintain its long-term productivity and contribute significantly to food security.

Analysis of past environment changes that resulted in dramatic famines (e.g. Ireland's potato famine and Ethiopia 1965–1997) shows specialised monocultures are highly vulnerable.

In addition to enhancing food security and climate resilience, diversity in the field also delivers important ecosystem services. Variety mixtures that are tolerant to drought and flood not only increase productivity, but also prevent soil erosion and desertification, increase soil organic matter and help stabilise slopes. Benefits for farmers include reducing the need for costly pesticides, receiving price premiums for valued traditional varieties and improving their dietary diversity and health.

Modern Breeding Techniques

In addition to increasing the diversity of crops and varieties in a single field, increasing the diversity of traits within one variety might help climate change adaptation. If each of the single varieties in one field has a higher tolerance to droughts, salinity, floods, storms and pests, the overall resilience to extreme weather events will be higher.

However, a review of the scientific literature reveals that the method of choice is not GE [genetic engineering], but traditional and modern conventional breeding techniques, including Marker Assisted Selection (MAS). There is considerable scope for breeding a large number of stress traits through the use of traditional varieties. These stress traits are generally regulated by multiple genes, which in turn are tightly controlled by complex interactions between genes, and between the plant and its environment. MAS facilitates the selection of conventional crosses with traits associated with multiple genes, including their as of yet unknown regulatory systems. By contrast, genetic engineering can only crudely insert a single or a few gene(s) without any control over regulatory mechanisms.

In recent years, MAS has yielded breeding successes, including some plants with traits that might be relevant for climate change resilience, such as drought, heat or cold resistant plants. However, it should be emphasised that none of these varieties alone will be able to contribute to food security in a changing climate. For erratic weather with rapid sequences of droughts, floods, storms and heat waves, only a mixed cropping system using a range of crops and varieties can provide the necessary diversity and resilience.

Breeding Successes

Some remarkable MAS successes:

- Rice tolerant to unpredictable floods. Rice production can be subject to stresses such as seasonal flooding, which can be unpredictable and can damage young rice plants. Through genetic mapping researchers identified a DNA segment containing a gene that makes rice tolerant to prolonged submergence in water. Using MAS, they successfully bred this trait into local and hybrid varieties. This allows the breeding of new varieties resilient to the erratic flooding that may occur as weather patterns become less predictable.

- One expected effect of climate change is the spread of disease. A new strain of wheat stem rust (Ug99), a fungus that can devastate wheat crops, is spreading across Africa. Most cultivated wheat varieties are susceptible to this virulent strain and efforts are underway to develop resistant wheat using MAS. The technique was chosen over GE due to MAS's ability to assist the breeding of complex traits. The breeding programme will use wheat's genetic diversity to find resistance genes that can be bred into high yielding varieties. This shows the importance of preserving the genetic diversity of crops, which are at risk because modern intensive agriculture relies on very few varieties.

Even Monsanto, the global genetic engineering giant, features this breeding technique in its R&D brochure and states under the heading 'Marker Assisted Breeding': "Today, the use of breakthrough technology has reinvented plant breeding so we can more than double the rate of 'genetic gain' in seeds—the improvement in important characteristics such as yield and tolerance to environmental stress."

These examples are evidence that it is possible to transfer plants' complex traits, including their regulatory systems, to commercial varieties using traditional breeding techniques assisted by genetic markers. In contrast to this, GE plants have so far failed to deliver on any of the decade-old promises on stress tolerance. Instead, current GE varieties are particularly susceptible to extreme weather.

The Limits of Genetic Engineering

So far, GE crops are restricted to a few traits that were developed some 20 years ago: herbicide and insect resistance. No stress tolerant GE plants have ever been proven to work under real world conditions. The performance of existing GE varieties under climate stress is so far sobering:

- Extreme temperature fluctuations caused crop losses in Bt cotton in China. Researchers investigating the disaster said high temperatures (37 C) were most probably responsible for causing a drop in Bt concentrations in leaves. Other researchers found that temperature changes, especially a cool period early on in the growing season, caused a reduction in the insect toxicity of Bt.

- GE herbicide-resistant soybeans suffered unexpected losses in the US during very hot spring weather in 1998. Roundup Ready soybeans performed significantly worse than conventional varieties under conditions of heat stress. The GE soybean stems were more brittle and split more easily, thus allowing infection to enter.

- Herbicide tolerant GE soybeans currently on the market have been reported to have decreased yields of up to 10 percent compared to traditional varieties. Massive herbicide use in conjunction with these GE plants has already led to an increase in tolerant weed populations. For example, 34 cases of glyphosate resistance in nine species have been documented in the US since 2000. Now it is recommended farmers have to spray stronger formulas of herbicides, and mixtures of herbicides, adding to costs.

Even if GE might be able to deliver a heat tolerant plant in 10 or 20 years, what would happen to the plant under extreme cold conditions, unseasonable rain or drought? A single gene does not provide protection against a multitude of conditions.

Currently, most GE stress tolerant plants in the pipeline use a rather crude approach of over expressing a single gene throughout the plant's life cycle. This approach is no match for the whole genome network that controls gene expression in natural plants, where genes are switched on and off and moderated throughout the plant's lifetime. By contrast, the inserted gene in the GE plant is on all the time, in all parts of the plant, with no other control. It is like an air conditioner always running at full speed—which could prove deadly in winter.

In summary, GE plants:

- Will provide no security against extreme weather changes. In a best case scenario, they may be resistant to a single stress, such as heat or drought, but not to the expected rapid and radical weather changes;

- Will lack any sophisticated regulation of the inserted gene and thus cannot respond to changing challenges;

- Because of their higher price, they will most likely be planted in monocultures, which have the highest risk of failing in changeable and extreme weather.

Given genetic engineering's limitations and our limited knowledge about plants' regulated response to environmental stress, unregulated single-trait GE crops are a threat to food security in a changing climate. The prospect of large monocultures of GE plants failing completely under unforeseen weather events is a recipe for disaster.

A one-sided focus on GE plants contradicts all scientific findings on climate change adaptation in agriculture, and is a long-term threat to global food security.

Proven Strategies

Bio-diverse farming is a proven, effective strategy to adapt to climate change. Through it we can create farms that are able to maintain and increase food production in the face of increasingly unpredictable conditions. In contrast, GE has inherent shortcomings pertaining to plant-environment interactions and complex gene regulations that make it unlikely to address climate change either reliably or in the long-term. This conclusion is also reflected in the recent IAASTD [International Assessment of Agriculture Science and Technology for Development] report, which considered GE crops to be irrelevant to achieving the Millennium Development Goals and to eradicating hunger.

Agriculture will not only be negatively affected by climate change, it is a substantial contributor to greenhouse gas emissions. By reducing agriculture's greenhouse gas emissions and by using farming techniques that increase soil carbon, farming itself can contribute to mitigating climate change. In fact, many biodiverse farming systems are both mitigation and adaptation strategies, as they increase soil carbon and use cropping systems that are more resilient to extreme weather.

In order to increase our food security in a changing climate, policy makers need to follow the IAASTD's recommendations and invest more in agricultural R&D that is geared towards modern, effective, bio-diverse farming. A one-sided focus on GE plants contradicts all scientific findings on climate change adaptation in agriculture, and is a long-term threat to global food security.

12

Regulating Corporate Land Purchases Will Reduce Food Insecurity

Logan Cochrane

Logan Cochrane is founder of Working to Empower, a Canadian organization that empowers youth to become involved in HIV & AIDS education projects and supports a children's home that cares for orphans living with HIV/AIDS. He also works with community-based organizations in seven African nations.

Food sovereignty—the right of people to own and manage local food systems—is closely connected to food security. Land grabs—the mass purchase of agricultural land by transnational companies—are displacing and disenfranchising local people, putting their food security at risk. These companies export most of the food harvested from land grabs to feed others, and locals must buy food rather than harvest it for themselves. Some claim that land grabs are a form of colonialism, but others add that local governments also contribute by encouraging land purchases. To protect the food security of vulnerable people, policymakers should regulate land grabs and support better local governance. To encourage these changes, communities must resist dispossession from their land.

The difference between food security and food sovereignty may seem like mere semantics, but in the hyper-globalized world wherein transnational companies may privately own significant portions of arable land in countries facing food insecurity, it is not just a matter of word play. . . .

Unequal Access to Food

Disparity of wealth and land ownership is not a new phenomenon. However, the degree to which agricultural lands are owned within areas of food insecurity makes food sovereignty as vital a factor as food security. An analysis of these concepts and their global implications is pressing, as over 963 million people do not have enough to eat. Most of them live in developing countries, and sixty-five percent of them live in only seven countries: China, India, Bangladesh, the Democratic Republic of Congo, Indonesia, Pakistan and Ethiopia. Furthermore, each year more people die due to hunger and malnutrition than to AIDS, tuberculosis, and malaria combined.

[T]he degree to which agricultural lands are owned within areas of food insecurity makes food sovereignty as vital a factor as food security.

The World Food Summit, held in 1996, declared that ideal food security includes the global population, whereby all people have access to sufficient, safe and nutritious food, encompassing both the physical availability and the economic access. The United Nations Universal Declaration of Human Rights and the Convention on the Rights of the Child both stipulate that it is the intrinsic right of all people to have access to food. However, the responsibility to enact these rights rests mostly on the nation-state, not the international community. On the other hand, some argue that repeated affirmations of human rights within the international realm do imply some global responsibility. The theoretical ideal is, therefore, that food security exists when all people in all places have access to sufficient, safe and nutritious food. Clearly that theoretical aim has not been met. Furthermore, if current mechanisms are not facilitating the aim it may require consideration of entirely new models of how countries engage with one another.

Defining Food Security and Sovereignty

Typical measurement of food security is limited to a specific place, such as a nation, city or household. USAID uses the household as a measurement, whereas the Food and Agriculture Organization (FAO) programs are nationally operated, thus limiting the global goals and human rights to the nation-state. Food insecurity also exists in differing levels. One person maybe facing a temporary bout of food insecurity, called "transitory", while another maybe consistently facing it, known as "chronic" food insecurity. Chronic food insecurity leads to high levels of vulnerability to hunger and famine. The achievement of food security does not necessitate that a country produce sufficient food supplies; but rather that a country is able to provide sufficient safe and nutritious food for its population. Thus, arises the question of food sovereignty: in a world of great economic disparity, will the food supplies of one region be given to another, even in the case where the local population faces chronic food insecurity?

Food security means the availability and access to sufficient safe food, whereas food sovereignty involves both ownership and the rights of local people to define local food systems, without first being subject to international market concerns. An important distinction must be made between food sovereignty as a theoretical construct and food sovereignty as a movement. The food sovereignty movement considers that the practices of multi-national corporations are akin to colonization, as such companies buy up large tracts of land and turn local agricultural resources into export cash-crops. As a movement, food sovereignty lacks direction and involves a great diversity of opinion and idea. As a model to re-consider and re-evaluate food, it highlights important challenges and offers potential remedies to current challenges. Food sovereignty as a theoretical construct, which is the definition that will be used throughout this paper, relates to the ownership and rights of food growers and local communities.

A Global Concern

Food security and food sovereignty are increasingly of global importance, with concerns not limited just to the developing world. In the 2008 price spike, consumers in Great Britain saw a fifteen-percent rise in average food items, while the BBC tracked some items increasing in cost by more than forty-percent. In the twelve month period before the price spike, the cost of wheat increased by 130% and rice by 74%. The pinch of paying more for food in developed countries was expressed differently in many developing countries, such as the mass rioting in Yemen, Somalia, Senegal, Pakistan, Mozambique, Indonesia, India, Egypt, Ivory Coast, Cameroon, Haiti, Burkina Faso, the Philippines and Bangladesh. At the same time, the World Resources Institute records sustainable and consistent increases in per capita food production over the last several decades.

USAID argues that food insecurity is often a result of poverty, while ownership, land rights and sovereignty are not mentioned as causal factors. While it is true that a direct relationship can be found between those who face food insecurity and those who are impoverished, that does not exclude other causes; such as, a lack of sovereignty or oppressive external factors. However, USAID does not take poverty alleviation and/or human rights as its prime reasons for engagement; rather its prime interests are to protect America and to create opportunities for Americans.

The European Union community has sought the improvement of food security for the least-developed countries through a plethora of national and international development bodies, while also engaging in massive export-based land acquisitions in those same regions. Ironically, the aim of reaching the Millennium Development Goals (MGDs) with funding and support from the European Union is countered by European Union businesses as they engage in activities that displace and dispossess locals of their land and livelihood. Increasing commercial production does not mean an increase of local or national food security, in particular when these foreign companies are exporting entire crops. This may in fact, lead to increased food insecurity and higher levels of malnutrition and poverty. Surprisingly, even Harvard University has used its investments in land-acquisition deals.

The Problem of "Land Grabbing"

A "land grab" refers to those land acquisitions that have caused displacement, dispossession and disenfranchisement; or, according to the Institute of Development Studies, it may also more broadly refer to the mass purchasing of agricultural lands by transnational companies. Land grabbing is occurring on a scale and at a rate faster than ever known before. When over one-hundred papers were presented at the International Conference on Global Land Grabbing in 2011, not one positive outcome could be found for local communities; such as, food security, employment and environmental sustainability. When such acquisitions occur in places of conflict, post-conflict and/or weak governance there is less monitoring and control and even greater negative impacts. Furthermore, large-scale land deals increase local food insecurity, as arable land produce is exported rather than reaching the local market; and smallholder farmers must purchase foods as opposed to harvesting it on their lands.

Lester Brown (2011) argues that land purchasing is a part of the global struggle to ensure food security. Food-importing countries are securing overseas supplies by attempting to control the entire supply-chain of food-stuffs, and thus avoid any potential problems that may arise in the process. Furthermore, he notes, that these deals are not only about food security but also water security. Countries such as Saudi Arabia used to produce much higher levels of wheat internally; however, due to declines in available fresh water these land deals have secured required sources of both food and water. [P.] Woodhouse and [A.S.] Ganho argue that the role played by water access in land grabs cannot be under-estimated, including the competition between local and investor in acquiring access to water resources and to sustainable water usage, as well as coping with the problems of creating pollution and chemical run-off. Case studies in Ethiopia demonstrate that access to, and rights of, water sources disproportionately favor investors over local smallholder farmers.

[L]arge-scale land deals increase local food insecurity, as arable land produce is exported rather than reaching the local market. . . .

The United Nations director of the Food and Agriculture Organization (FAO) called these land-lease deals 'neo-colonialist. This statement was echoed by US Secretary of State Hillary Clinton, who warned of a new wave of colonialism. [English journalist] Madeleine Bunting envisions a "dystopian future in which millions of the hungry are excluded from the land of their forefathers by barbed wire fences and security guards as food is exported to feed the rich world." The wider view must, however, include the role of local/national government in facilitating, and in some cases encouraging, the sale of arable land and displacement of peoples. Other analysts have more cautiously labeled the vast selling of agricultural lands to investors as the third wave of outsourcing. The first wave consisted of investors looking for locations with cheaper labour. The second wave was the out-sourcing of middle-class jobs to places such as India because of its advances in information technology. This may be the third wave:

the out-sourcing of growing and harvesting of food supplies to locations where there is cheap fertile land. . . .

Case Study: Ethiopia

In contrast to [the] rosy predictions [by Ethiopian Prime Minister Meles Zenawi], USAID, which is one of Ethiopia's largest donors ($600 million of food aid in 2009-10), outlines that successful agricultural development and food security requires "100% ownership and buy-in by the Ethiopian people" (USAID, 2010, p. 5). And yet, the Ethiopian government and transnational corporations are doing exactly the opposite, in displacing and dispossessing Ethiopians and handing over control and ownership to non-local corporations and governments. *The Economist* (2009) highlighted an interesting parallel in the $100-million Saudi investment to grow and export rice, wheat and barley on a 99-year land-lease in Ethiopia, while the United Nations World Food Program plans to spend $116-million, over a five-year period, providing emergency food aid to Ethiopia. In 2008 the Ethiopian famine was compounded as food continued to be exported and did not reach the local market (Dominguez, 2010). Yet fertile Ethiopian agricultural land continues to be leased for as little as $1 per acre (Bunting, 2011).

According to Ethiopian government sources, over thirty-six countries have leased land within its borders (Vidal, 2011). Although estimates vary, it is thought that 60–80% of food production in Ethiopia is completed by women. Thus the role of gender is revealed by analysis of those affected by land sales and dispossessions (USAID, 2010). Of those who face the brunt of food shortages and insecurity in Ethiopia, most are women and children (USAID, 2010). Furthermore, areas of large-scale plantations are more likely to be poverty-affected than prosperous in respect to the local populations (Da Via, E. 2011). As a parallel example, case studies from Cambodia show that land grabs do not benefit local residents, and over time resulted in collective action by the local population against political and commercial interests (Schneider, 2011).

The massive land-lease deals are not without their supporters, however. The technology transfer, increase in number of jobs and foreign investment are usually cited as having positive effects for the overall benefit of Ethiopia and its citizens. Ethiopian Ambassador to the UK, Berhanu Kabede (2011), published a response [in 2011] arguing that land-leases assist Ethiopia to move towards mechanized agriculture to increase production capability, and as such the government has set aside 7.4 million acres of agricultural land for land-lease deals. The Ambassador further notes that this is only a portion of Ethiopia's arable land (ibid). The Ambassador highlights some of the positive environmental changes the Ethiopian government has made in recent years, including the planting of 1-billion trees, re-foresting 15-million hectares of land and a national plan to become carbon neutral by 2025 (ibid).

Ambassador Kabede did not mention some of the negative impacts the vast land sales will have; such as, displacement of local farmers, uncompensated dispossession of their land, continued food scarcity as investors export what is grown, unsustainable resource use, and environmental damage to lands, atmosphere and water. Furthermore, the majority of the world's poor are rural dwellers who engage in some small-scale farming. As a result of the dispossession of land and displacement of people, poverty levels will increase and more people will be forced to migrate away from agricultural areas to city-centers. World Bank studies (Riddell, 2007) confirm that the push for macro-economic development via liberalization of markets has detrimental effects on particular groups of society, particularly the poor.

Guillozet and Bliss (2011) found that, although investment in the forestry sector is low in Ethiopia, the agricultural investments affect natural forests by mass clearing and burning.

As a result, there are long-term negative impacts. Biodiversity is currently being reduced by the cutting and burning of hundreds of hectares of forest, as well as by the draining of swamps and marshlands (Vidal, 2011). Pesticides have also been shown, in Ethiopian cases, to kill bees and other unintended flora and fauna. Beyond the investment land itself the clearing of natural forests is affecting livelihoods on a much larger scale, by negatively affecting the wider ecosystems (Guillozet and Bliss, 2011).

Such deals are neither agricultural development nor rural development, but simply agribusiness development, according to GRAIN (2008). An unpublished report that interviewed 150 local farm households in Ethiopia found that there is weak monitoring of investor activities from regional and national government. It also found that accelerated forest degradation resulted in loss of livelihood security for community members. Furthermore, in Cameroon, cases of land grabs demonstrate that the transnational investment in agriculture is a major obstacle to local livelihoods, traditional resource ownership and land rights, as well as to sustainable development (Simo, 2011). In yet another example, Rwandan land grabs have shown the move from traditionally owned and operated farms into large-scale corporate mono-crop cultivation has negatively affected livelihoods through loss of land as well as means of financial security, resulting in increased poverty levels and food insecurity despite overall macro-economic gains (Ansom, 2011). . . .

[L]and-lease deals are becoming more commonplace, with large sales in Sudan, Egypt, Congo, Zambia, Mali, Sierra Leone, Tanzania, Kenya, Madagascar, Liberia, Ghana, and Mozambique. Although there are land deals taking place outside of Africa, over 50% of the estimated 60–80 million hectares of such deals in the last three years took place there, approximately an area the size of France. The largest land buyers include China, India, South Korea, the United Arab Emirates and Saudi Arabia; yet some of the largest deals are done with Western funding. Cases from Sierra Leone show that a lack of knowledge-sharing with locals, along with a plethora of false promises, has led to social, environmental and economic loss. Addax Bioenergy received the use of 40,000 hectares to grow ethanol for export to the European Union (EU). Local villagers were in turn promised two-thousand jobs and environmental protection of the swamps. However, three years into the project only fifty jobs materialized, while some of the swamps have been drained and others damaged by irrigation. Those jobs that did exist paid USD $2.50 per day on a casual basis. Clearly these are not isolated cases and action is required to stem the tsunami of sales of land in food-insecure areas.

Making Recommendations

Re-evaluate the system: Up to twenty-five percent of crops are lost due to pests and diseases and the developing world loses up to an additional thirty-seven percent of harvested foods due to problems in storage and transportation. Every day 4.4 million apples, 5.1 million potatoes, 2.8 million tomatoes and 1.6 million bananas are thrown in the garbage. Systematic shifts that address this loss may focus upon local sustainability and buy local movements, rather than relying upon export commodities and global transport for the sale and supply of food stuffs. This requires participation that includes local ownership and collective decision making.

Provide Sustainable Solutions: Much of modern agriculture is mechanized, using oil-based chemical fertilizers, pesticides and herbicides. This system of agriculture is not sustainable. It needs to be remedied with a more sustainable approach to agriculture—which can be just as agriculturally productive. On example of how sustainable initiatives can be promoted and supported is the Equator Initiative, which provides financial prizes and knowledge sharing for community-driven efforts that reduce poverty through sustainable use of biodiversity. . . .

Regulate Land Grabbing: The World Bank has proposed guidelines, but does not have the means or authority to enforce them. In order for guidelines to be enforced, such as those developed by the World Bank, national governments must be involved, for this to take place greater coordination on the international level and advocacy from the NGO [nongovernmental organization] and public sectors is required. Madagascar demonstrates the power of collective action, as does Sudan and Cambodia, yet long-term and effective change will require governmental enforced regulation.

Establish Good Governance: The purchasing of land and forced displacement of peoples occurs not solely due to transnational pressure, but with government approval. Citizens and the international community must encourage, and work towards, better governance decisions. An international framework for responsible investing could be created. However, such a framework would remain weak and ineffective unless adopted and enforced by national governments. In order to ensure that investments are beneficial for both the investor and the community, this framework must ensure food security and livelihood protection for the local communities. Further encouragement can be levied on governance in tying good governance to official development assistance; such systems have been developed and enacted by the World Bank and others.

Monitor and Penalize Environmental Damage: Companies must be more strictly monitored with regard to environmental damage, both by the public and private sectors. Monitoring and evaluation of investments ought to be strengthened with regulation and policy by the relevant national government and by international bodies. NGOs and communities can take inspiration from others who have taken transnational companies to court, and won. National government need to recognize the short-term benefits do not out-weigh the long-term environmental damage, and seek compensation to rectify violations. The scale of land acquisitions demonstrate that such regulations will likely not significantly deter investments and investors, as efforts to do so in Tanzania demonstrate.

[T]he forced relocation of rural farmers will likely increase the numbers of people living in poverty . . . [and] the numbers of people in need of emergency food aid.

Develop Rural Agriculture: Currently less than one percent of smallholder farmers use irrigation techniques in Ethiopia. An improvement in this regard will allow for increased productivity as well as year-round water availability. Facilitation of loans for the purchase of pumps (as smallholder farmers often lack financial resources to make such investments), as well as access to internal markets with infrastructural developments can improve community-driven and locally-owned productivity.

Undertake Land Reform: Changes on the national level will require land reforms, ownership reforms and recognition of traditional land rights. Such land reforms and rights have been evolving in Madagascar, following the rejection of the Daewod land-grab deal and the installation of a new government. Tanzania has also enacted progressive rights for recognizing traditional land title. . . .

As highlighted by the Ethiopian case study, it becomes readily apparent that the forced relocation of rural farmers will likely increase the numbers of people living in poverty. Consequently, there will be an increase in the numbers of people in need of emergency food aid. Aggregate data on food security will not measure the importance of food sovereignty, nor do the data take into account unjust practices and environmental damage. The majority of Ethiopians are subsistence farmers, and depriving them of their land, rights and livelihood neglects the importance of human rights and environmental protection. One means to achieve the goal of national food security, as well as a reduction of required emergency food aid, is to increase effectiveness of rural farms.

The prospect of attaining sovereignty over land and the food grown on it encourages smallholder farmers to continue their livelihood while seeking to increase overall food security.

Engaging in Community Resistance

Communities themselves must engage and be active in resisting forced relocation and dispossession of their land and rights. Examples of such resistance include that of Madagascar and the Southern Sudanese movement, which advocates land belongs to the community and requires its involvement, as well as active community resistance to land grabs in Cambodia. Communities must seek to be participants in the discussion, to be involved in the process and to voice their concerns. Food security of the wealthy at the expense of the impoverished will not work and requires new approaches. The prospect of attaining sovereignty over land and the food grown on it encourages smallholder farmers to continue their livelihood while seeking to increase overall food security.

[According to D. Vhugen, in a 2011 article in *The Economist*], "In most poor nations, there are large gaps between actual and potential agricultural yields. But the best route to closing this gap usually is not super-sized farms. In most labour-intensive agricultural settings, small farms are more productive than large farms. They could become even more productive—and as a result likely minimise unrest—if developing country governments provide these family farms with secure land rights that allow farmers to invest in their own land and improve their harvests."

The World Bank's 2010 report found that land grabs ignored proper legal procedures, displaced local peoples without compensation, encroached on areas beyond the agreement, had negative impacts on gender disparity, were environmentally destructive, provided far fewer jobs than promised, leased land below market value and routinely excluded pastoralists and displaced peoples from consultations. Furthermore, the World Bank concludes: "many investments . . . failed to live up to expectations and, instead of generating sustainable benefits, contributed to asset loss and left local people worse off than they would have been without the investment." . . .

13

Empowering Women Will Reduce Food Insecurity

Juhie Bhatia

Juhie Bhatia, a reporter and editor, is currently the public health editor at Global Voices Online *and the managing editor at* Women's eNews. *She covers health and women's issues and has written for* Reuters Health, Bust, HealthDay, Bulletin for the World Health Organization, *MSNBC.com*, iVillage, Natural Health, *and Planned Parenthood's teenwire.com.*

Giving women greater control over food production will reduce food insecurity. Although women produce 50 percent of the world's food, few recognize their efforts. Providing women with the same agricultural tools and financial access as men would increase agricultural production in developing countries. In many communities, because women cannot own land, they cannot access the resources they need to feed their families. Moreover, some male farmers discourage the participation of their wives. Thus, policies that allow women to own property and increased education about the importance of women in agricultural production would reduce food insecurity. Where women are given ownership and control, food production increases.

A s global food prices continue to remain high, with potential increases on the horizon because of soaring oil prices and supply concerns, experts says there is one often-overlooked solution for fighting hunger: women.

Juhie Bhatia, "Is Empowering Women Key to Eradicating Global Hunger?," *Global Voices Online*, Pulitzer Center on Crisis Reporting, April 13, 2011. Used under Creative Commons License.

A Gender Gap

Women are vital to food production in many developing countries, making up on average 43 percent of the agricultural labor force. Some estimate that 80 percent of those involved in farming in Africa and 60 percent in Asia are women.

At the Envision forum last week [April 2011] in New York City, during a panel focused on women's roles in alleviating hunger and poverty, United Nations Development Programme Under-Secretary General and Associate Administrator Rebeca Grynspan said:

> Even talking only about the rural areas, women produce 50 percent of the food of the world. They receive only 1 percent of the credit but they produce 50 percent of the food.

In addition to a lack of recognition, a report released last month from the United Nation's (UN) Food and Agriculture Organization says that while female farmers' roles may vary across regions, they consistently have less access to resources and opportunities than their male counterparts. Closing this gender gap could lift as many as 150 million people out of hunger.

Ma. Estrella A. Penunia, posting on the website of the Asian Farmers Association for Sustainable Rural Development, lists six key reasons why we should care about female farmers, including food security issues. Meanwhile, Emily Oakley, a United States (U.S.) farmer who has studied small-scale farming in dozens of countries, reflects in a post on the blog *In Her Field* on women in agriculture:

> In most places I have visited, women are more than just supporters of agriculture; they partner with their husbands in day-to-day tasks, decision-making, and planning. In Kenya, it is far more typical to see a woman by herself with a child strapped on her back turning up a field with a hoe in hand than it is to see her joined by her husband. In a remote village of Western Nepal (the kind of remote that

means half a day's walk to the nearest road), the farmer everyone in town agreed was most innovative was a woman. Her farm stood out on the hillside as an oasis of growth and diversity where other farms were experiencing soil erosion and poor yields. I recently participated in a farmer-to-farmer project in the Dominican Republic focusing on women farmers in commercial hoop house production of bell peppers. This is just the tiniest taste of women's work in agriculture.

Closing [the] gender gap could lift as many as 150 million people out of hunger.

Food for the Whole Family

Many women work as subsistence farmers, small-scale entrepreneurs, unpaid workers or casual wage laborers. Giving these women the same tools and resources as men, including better access to financial services, technical equipment, land, education and markets, could increase agricultural production in developing countries by 2.5 to 4 percent, according to the UN report. These production gains could, in turn, reduce the number of hungry people by 12 to 17 percent, or by 100 to 150 million people. There were roughly 925 million undernourished people globally in 2010.

Empowering women could also improve food security for their entire family, says the report, because women are more likely than men to spend additional income on food, education and other basic household needs. But Dipendra Pokharel, a researcher in Nepal, says on his blog that women's roles in the home can also mean their needs get overlooked:

Women farmers often have different priorities than their male counterparts, and this can, in many cases, be related to their direct role in feeding their family. In the rural areas of Nepal, traditionally men control the outside world and women the inside of the home. Such traditional perspectives can contribute to the lop-sidedness of 'gender blind' information, collected by outsiders with the intention of helping a community. It is usually the men who provide information to the outsiders. This means that women's priorities are often overlooked, unless they are specifically taken into account. This also supports the view that the female farmers receive less extension services which are needed to transform their subsistence-based farming system to a more commercial one.

Female farmers operate smaller farms than male farmers, on average only half to two-thirds as large, according to the report, and their farms usually have lower yields. They are also less likely to own land or have access to rented land. The report shows, for example, that women represent fewer than 5 percent of all agricultural holders in West Asia and North Africa.

Jane Tarh Takang, who has worked with farmers in West and Central Africa, discusses land rights issues in an interview by Edith Abilogo posted on *FORESTSBlog*, the blog of The Center for International Forestry Research:

> In most communities in Africa, women and girls have very limited access to property and land compared with boys and men. Without land, they cannot produce resources to feed their family or generate income, and this results in extending the poverty cycle to their children. This situation is worse when it comes to widows or unmarried women . . . In cases where the existing farmlands have been depleted due to unsustainable agricultural practices, men would prefer to reserve the fertile areas for their own use and leave the less fertile ones to the women.

Elfinesh Dermeji, an Ethiopian female farmer who attended the Workshop on Gender and Market-Oriented Agriculture in Addis Ababa earlier this year, says in a post on the *New Agriculturist* that it is not always easy to get women involved in agriculture:

In some families when the men are positive and they want their wives to participate, the woman is not business oriented or she's not motivated. On the other side there are some men, when women are motivated and they want to participate, they don't want her to leave the house. They would rather not have that income than have their wife involved in an association.

A Search for Solutions

Still, numerous projects globally are involving female farmers, from encouraging women in Ghana to buy tractors to lobbying the Philippines government to allow the wife's name on land titles to increasing the use of information and communication technologies among Ugandan farmers.

On *OneWorld South Asia*, Ananya Mukherjee-Reed describes how 250,000 Kudumbashree members, a network of 3.7 million women in the Indian state of Kerala, have formed farming collectives to jointly lease and cultivate land:

> 'As farmers, now we control our own time, resources and labour,' was the refrain I heard over and over again. Dhanalakhsmi, a young woman in Elappully, tells me that the change in her role from a labourer to producer has had a profound effect on her children. 'They see me differently now. When we are at meetings discussing our farms, our incomes, or simply sharing our problems, they watch with a lot of interest.'

But bloggers say more can be done. In a post on *Solutions*, Yifat Susskind argues that the U.S. should buy crops from local African farmers as part of their foreign aid. Dipendra Pokharel says rural women must gain social and political space in private and public domains. Melissa McEwan, blogging on *Shakesville* in the U.S., challenges the misconception that only men are farmers by compiling almost 100 photos of female farmers worldwide. The report says changes are also needed at the policy level.

Whatever the approach, Ma. Estrella A. Penunia says to truly succeed it should be inclusive:

> As farming in many developing countries is a family endeavor, the one important thing also that can greatly help women farmers is the support that they will get from their husbands and male leaders/members of their organizations. In households where both the man and the woman have been sensitized to the dynamics of gender and believe in equal rights and opportunities, the full potentials of a woman farmer are harnessed to the fullest.

Organizations to Contact

The editors have compiled the following list of organizations concerned with the issues debated in this book. The descriptions are derived from materials provided by the organizations. All have publications or information available for interested readers. The list was compiled on the date of publication of the present volume; the information provided here may change. Be aware that many organizations take several weeks or longer to respond to inquiries, so allow as much time as possible.

American Farm Bureau
600 Maryland Avenue, SW, Suite 1000W
Washington, DC   20024
(202) 406-3600
website: www.fb.org

The bureau is an independent organization that represents the interests of and advocates for US farmers. The goal of the bureau is to analyze problems facing agricultural producers and formulate solutions that create economic opportunities and promote social advancement, which will in turn improve the national well-being. On the organization's website are publications on topics that affect the agricultural community such as free trade policy, farm bills, agricultural chemicals, and food safety. Current issues and archives of the *FBNews*, a biweekly newsletter, are available on the bureau's website, as are news updates and a bureau blog.

Center for Global Food Issues
Hudson Institute, Churchville, VA   24421
(540) 337-6354 • fax: (540) 337-8593
website: www.cgfi.org

The center conducts research and provides analysis of agriculture and environmental concerns related to food production in order to heighten awareness of the connection between agricultural productivity and environmental conservation. With the goal of improving farmers' understanding of the new globalized farm economy, the center hopes to increase awareness of the environmental impact of various farming systems and food policies. The center promotes free trade and opposes limits on technological innovation in agriculture. On its website are publications related to this mission, including "Meeting the Needs of a Hungry World: What Role Does Biotechnology Play" and "Wages of Fear: the Costs to Society of Attacks on the Product of Human Ingenuity."

Center for Trade Policy Studies
CATO Institute, Washington, DC   20001-5403
(202) 842-0200 • fax: (202) 842-3490
e-mail: cato@cato.org
website: www.cato.org/trade-immigration

A project of the CATO Institute, a libertarian think tank, the center analyzes farm policies as an advocate of global free markets. The center opposes government interference and international policies that limit free trade. CATO publishes the quarterly magazine *Regulation*, the bimonthly *Cato Policy Report*, and numerous policy papers and articles. On its trade-immigration web link, CATO publishes multi-media resources and recent articles, including "The Benefits of Biotech," "It's Time to KickFamers off the Federal Dole," and "Food Fight."

Consultative Group on International Agricultural Research (CGIAR)
CGIAR Secretariat, The World Bank, MSN G6-601
Washington, DC   20433
(202) 473-8951 • fax: (202) 473-8110
e-mail: cigar@cgiar.org
website: www.cgiar.org

CGIAR is a global collaborative group of government and civic organizations and private businesses. The group makes its research available to individuals and organizations with the goal of improving food security to benefit the world's poor. It fosters sustainable agricultural growth, better human nutrition and health, higher incomes and improved management of natural resources. The group publishes joint publications, fact sheets, and reports from its research centers on its website, including *The CGAIR at 40 and Beyond: Impacts that Matter for the Poor and the Planet* and *Climate, Agriculture and Food Security: A Strategy for Change.*

Food First
Institute for Food and Development Policy
Oakland, CA   94618
(510) 654-4400 • fax: (510)654-4551
website: www.foodfirst.org

The mission of Food First is to influence public policy by examining the root causes of global hunger, poverty, and ecological degradation and to develop solutions, in partnership with social change movements, to eliminate the injustices that cause hunger. On its website the institute publishes backgrounders, policy briefs, reports, journal articles, stories, and field reports, including the backgrounder "Food Security, Food Justice, or Food Sovereignty?" and the policy brief. "Smallholder Solutions to Hunger, Poverty, and Climate Change."

International Food Policy Research Institute (IFPRI)
2033 K Street, NW, Washington, DC   20006-1002
(202) 862-5600 • fax: (202) 467-4439
e-mail: ifpri@cgiar.org
website: www.ifpri.org

IFPRI, a CGIAR (Consultative Group on International Agricultural Research) center, seeks sustainable solutions to end hunger and poverty by ensuring every person has secure access to sufficient and safe food to sustain a healthy and productive life. Its vision is to include consumers and producers in transparent food policy decisions. The institute publishes the annual *Global Hunger Index*, its quarterly magazine, *Insights*, and policy briefs. Available on its website are the *2011 Global Hunger Index*, the latest issue of *Insights*, and the policy briefs "Assessing the Land Use Change Consequences of European Biofuel Policies," and "Understanding the Linkage Between Agricultural Productivity and Nutrient Consumption."

Organization for Competitive Markets (OCM)
P.O. Box 6486, Lincoln, NE   68506
website: www.competitivemarkets.com

OCM is a think tank and advocacy group that promotes government-regulated free markets in agriculture. The organization believes that international trade agreements threaten national sovereignty while increasing the market power of global agribusinesses. OCM publishes a newsletter that documents its political activities and comments on US food policy. Recent and archived issues of the newsletter are available on its website.

US Agency for International Development (USAID)
Ronald Reagan Building, Washington, DC   20523-1000
(202) 712-4810 • fax: (202) 216-3524
website: www.usaid.gov

USAID extends assistance to the developing world and those countries recovering from disaster. The agency supports long-term and equitable economic growth. Although an independent federal government agency, its foreign policy guidance comes from the US Secretary of State. To advance US foreign policy goals, it supports economic growth, agriculture and trade, global health, conflict prevention, and humanitarian assistance. On its Public Affairs link, USAID provides access to news releases, fact sheets, speeches, testimony, and reports.

The World Bank
1818 H Street, NW, Washington, DC   20433
(202) 473-1000 • fax: (202) 477-6391
website: www.worldbank.org

The World Bank provides financial and technical assistance to developing countries worldwide. The bank provides low-interest loans, interest-free credits, and grants to developing countries for a wide array of purposes, including agriculture and environmental and natural resource management. The bank publishes two journals: *World Bank Research Observer* and *World Bank Economic Review*. On the website's Data & Research Link, the bank provides a searchable database of articles and reports, including *Land Policies for Growth and Poverty Reduction* and *Breaking the Conflict Trap: Civil War and Development Policy*.

World Food Programme (WPF)

Via C.G.Viola 68, Parco dei Medici, Rome   00148
   Italy
+39-06-65131 • fax: +39-06-6513 2840
website: www.wfp.org

The World Food Programme, the world's largest humanitarian organization, is an arm of the United Nations that fights global hunger. WFP's vision is of a world in which every man, woman, and child has equal access to food. Its food assistance reaches people in 80 countries every year. WPF publishes brochures, fact sheets, policy papers, strategic plans, speeches, and annual reports, many of which are available on its website, including its "World Hunger" series.

World Neighbors

4127 N.W. 122nd St., Oklahoma City, OK   73120
(405) 752-9700 • fax: (405) 752-9393
website: www.wn.org

World Neighbors is an international development organization whose goal is to eliminate hunger, poverty, and disease in poor, isolated rural villages in Asia, Africa, and Latin America. It does not give away food or material aid, but provides training and support to rural communities in developing countries to improve their farm yields and make other community improvements. The organization publishes *Neighbors*, a quarterly magazine, and an electronic newsletter, recent and archived issues of which are available on its website.

Bibliography

Books

Christopher B. Barrett and Daniel G. Maxwell	*Food Aid After Fifty Years: Recasting Its Role.* New York: Routledge, 2005.
Lester R. Brown	*Outgrowing the Earth: The Food Security Challenge in an Age of Falling Water Tables and Rising Temperatures.* New York: W.W. Norton, 2005.
Patrick Curry	*Ecological Ethics: An Introduction.* Malden, MA: Polity, 2011.
Simon Dresner	*Principles of Sustainability.* New York: Routledge, 2008.
Andres R. Edwards and David W. Orr	*Sustainability Revolution: Portrait of a Paradigm Shift.* Gabriola Island, BC: New Society, 2005.
Giovanni Federico	*An Economic History of World Agriculture, 1800–2000.* Princeton, NJ: Princeton University Press, 2005.
Basudeb Guha-Khasnobis, Shabd S. Acharya, and Benjamin Davis, eds.	*Food Insecurity, Vulnerability, and Human Rights Failure.* New York: Palgrave Macmillan, 2007.

John Ingram, Polly Ericksen, and Diana Liverman, eds.	*Food Security and Global Environmental Change.* New York: Routledge, 2010.
Tim Jackson	*Prosperity Without Growth: Economics for a Finite Planet.* New York: Routledge, 2011.
Eric Lichtfouse, ed.	*Genetics, Biofuels and Local Farming Systems.* New York: Springer, 2011.
Muriel Lightbourne	*Food Security, Biological Diversity, and Intellectual Property Rights.* Burlington, VT: Ashgate, 2009.
David B. Lobell and Marshal Burke, eds.	*Climate Change and Food Security: Adapting Agriculture to a Warmer World.* New York: Springer, 2009.
Robert Paarlberg	*Food Politics: What Everyone Needs to Know.* New York: Oxford University Press, 2010.
Michael Pollan	*The Omnivore's Dilemma: A Natural History of Four Meals.* New York: Penguin, 2007.
William D. Schanbacher	*Politics of Food: The Global Conflict Between Food Security and Food Sovereignty.* New York: Praeger, 2010.
D. John Shaw	*World Food Security: A History Since 1945.* New York: Palgrave Macmillan, 2007.
Paul B. Thompson	*Food Biotechnology in Ethical Perspective.* New York: Springer, 2007.

James Vernon   *Hunger: A Modern History.* Cambridge, MA: Harvard University Press, 2007.

Worldwatch Institute   *State of the World 2011: Innovations That Nourish the Planet.* New York: W.W. Norton, 2011.

Periodicals and Internet Sources

Walden Bello   "Manufacturing a Food Crisis," *Nation,* May 15, 2008.

Marcia Clemmitt   "Global Food Crisis," *CQ Researcher,* June 27, 2008.

Anne Laure Constantin   "A Time of High Prices: An Opportunity for the Rural Poor," Institute for Agriculture and Trade Policy, April 2008. www.iatp.org.

Christopher D. Cook   "Why Monsanto's GM Seeds Threaten Democracy," *Christian Science Monitor,* February 23, 2011.

Tom Daschle   "Food Security Has Global Implications," *Politico,* June 7, 2011.

The Economist   "The New Face of Hunger," April 19, 2008.

Lynette Evans   "Pollan Preaches Sustainability to Garden Lovers," *San Francisco Chronicle,* September 30, 2006.

Leslie Leyland Fields	"A Feast Fit for the King: Returning Growing Fields and Kitchen Table to God," *Christianity Today*, November 2010.
Foreign Policy	"Threats to Food Security," March/April 2010.
Justin Gillis	"A Warming Planet Struggles to Feed Itself," *New York Times*, June 4, 2011.
Daniel Griswold	"Grain Drain: The Hidden Cost of U.S. Rice Subsidies," Cato Institute, November 2006. www.freetrade.org /node/539.
Guardian [UK]	"Food Security: Bread and Freedom," February 1, 2011.
Jim Harkness	"Food Security and National Security," Institute for Agriculture and Trade Policy, March 8, 2011. www.iatp.org.
Dean Kleckner	"Farmers Want to Feed the World—Let Them Do It!," truth abouttrade.org, June 30, 2011.
Ross Korves	"Technology to Feed the World," truthabouttrade.org, June 16, 2011.
Marc Lacey	"Across Globe, Empty Bellies Bring Rising Anger," *New York Times*, April 18, 2008.
Danielle Nierenberg	"Corporate Land Grabs Threaten Food Security," *Worldwatch*, August 2, 2011.

Romano Pradi   "Biofuels Can't Feed Starving People," *Christian Science Monitor,* April 29, 2008.

Randy Schnepf   "High Agricultural Commodity Prices: What Are the Issues?," *Congressional Research Service,* May 6, 2008.

Science Daily   "Food Insecurity Associated with Developmental Risk in Children," January 16, 2008.

Science Daily   "One Billion Hungry People: Multiple Causes of Food Insecurity Considered," July 14, 2009.

Barrett Sheridan   "Blame It on Biofuels," *Newsweek International,* August 20, 2007.

USAID's Infant & Young Child Nutrition Project   *Nutrition and Food Security Impacts of Agriculture Projects: A Review of Experience,* February 2011. www .usaid.gov.

Index

A

Abilogo, Edith, 116
Absenteeism, 27, 107
Academic achievement and hunger, 26
"Access" pillar of food security, 13, 31, 51
Addax Bioenergy, 108
Africa
    agriculture, 18–19, 77–78, 82–84, 110
    armed conflicts, 33–35
    climate change, 15, 52–53
    corporate land purchases, 104, 105–107, 107, 110–111
    countries needing assistance programs, 40
    food production, 76, 82
    food riots, 41, 102
    hunger increase, 14, 75, 100
    irrigation, 78, 82, 110
    malnutrition, 53
    rainfall, 90
    wheat stem rust, 95
    wildlife conservation, 63
    women, 114, 116, 117
Agency for International Development, 83
Agriculture
    aid, 32, 36, 75–78, 82–84, 110
    barriers, 9
    corporate land purchases, 99–112
    disinterest, 14, 15
    implementation policies, 9
    industrial, 8
    land use, 7–8, 67

precision farming, 81
    research funding, 17, 20–21, 98
    technology can decrease food insecurity, 9, 58, 75–78, 81, 85–88, 106, 110
    technology is greener, 80–82
    See also Biotechnology; Crop yields
Aid programs. *See* Assistance programs
AIDS, 24, 54
Algae, 22
Algeria, 41
Alley, Marcus, 9
Alternative fuels. *See* Biofuels
American Journal of Clinical Nutrition, 79
Animal feed, 8
Aquaculture, 21, 23–24, 72
Arabian oryx, 62, 63
Armed conflicts, 30–36, 103
Asia
    armed conflicts, 35
    birth rates, 71
    climate change, 15, 52
    food riots, 102
    Green Revolution, 13, 76–77
    hunger increase, 14, 75
    rainfall, 90
    wildlife, 62
    women, 114, 116, 117
    See also China; India
Asian Farmers Association for Sustainable Rural Development, 114